Feathered Critter Friends
Vol. III

Feathered Critter friends

Vol. III

Rob Benton

Esotericom®

All birds depicted herein were photographed in the course of their natural behavior. No bird was enticed, confined, entrapped, or harassed in any way in the making of these photographs.

Captions indicate general identification of the bird and where the photograph was made.

Front cover: Kookaburra
Back cover: Forest Red-Tailed Black Cockatoos

All photographs by Rob Benton

ISBN 978-0-9980682-1-3

"Surely in vain
the net is spread
in the sight of any bird..."

Proverbs 1:17

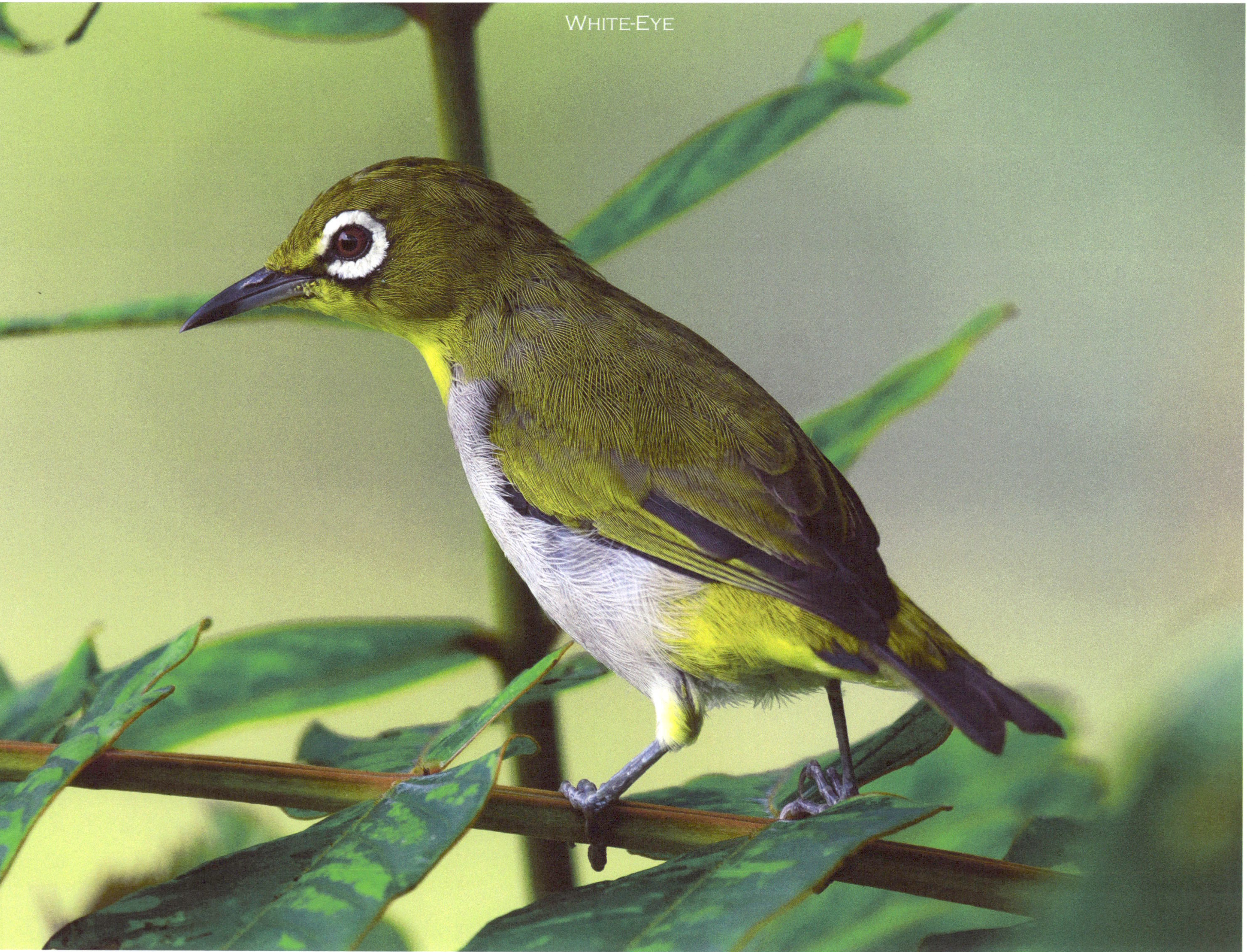

White-Eye

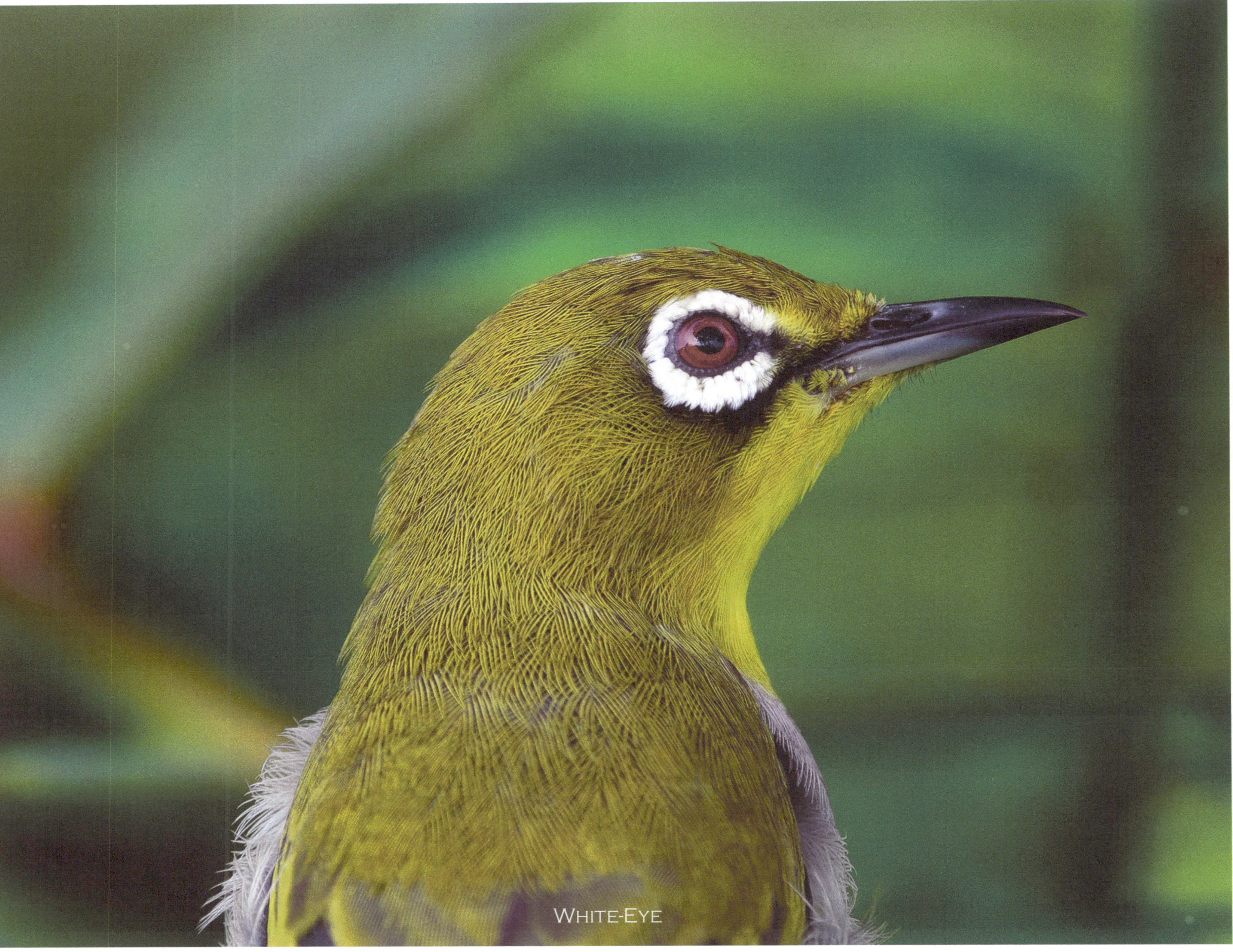
White-Eye

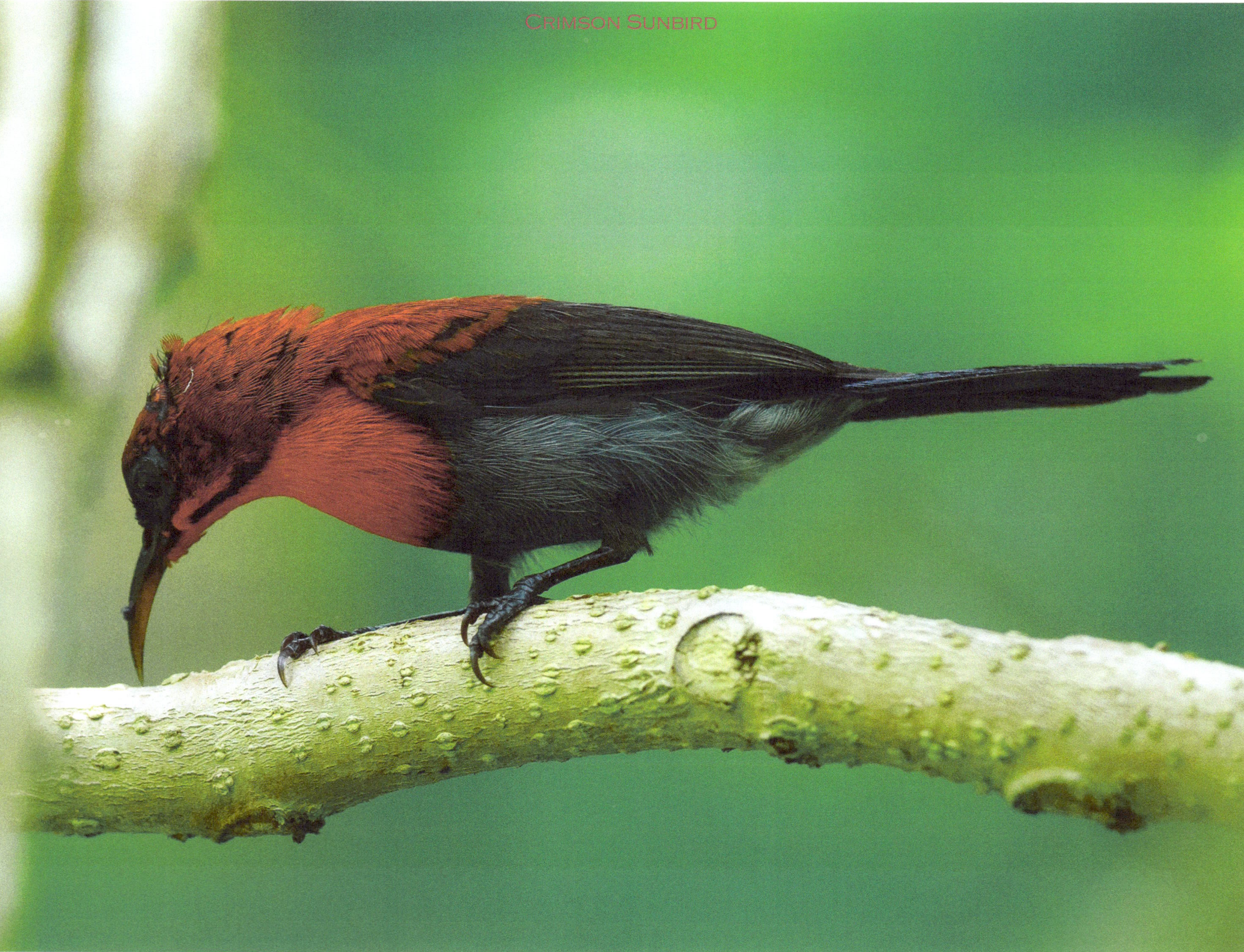

Crimson Sunbird

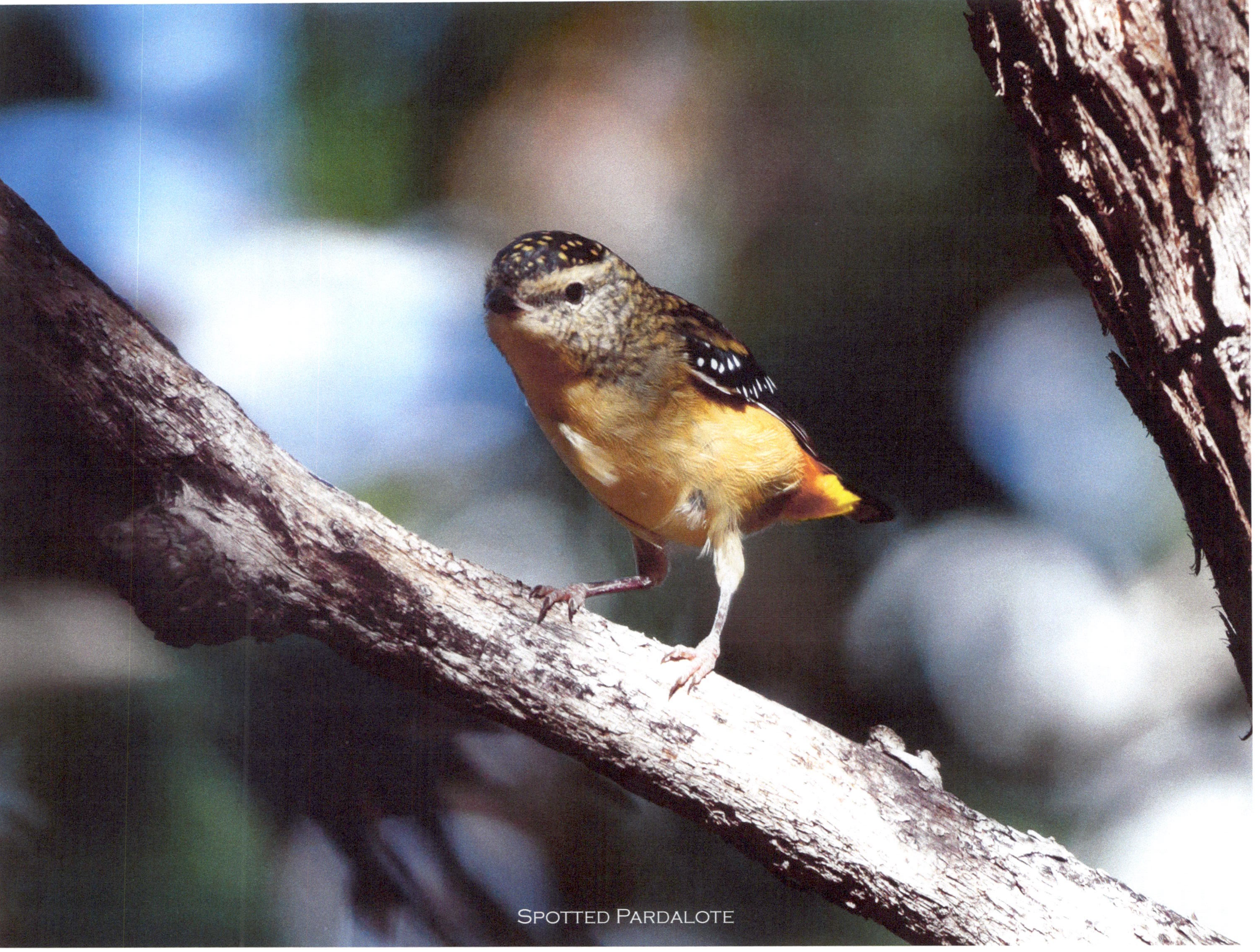

Spotted Pardalote

GULL

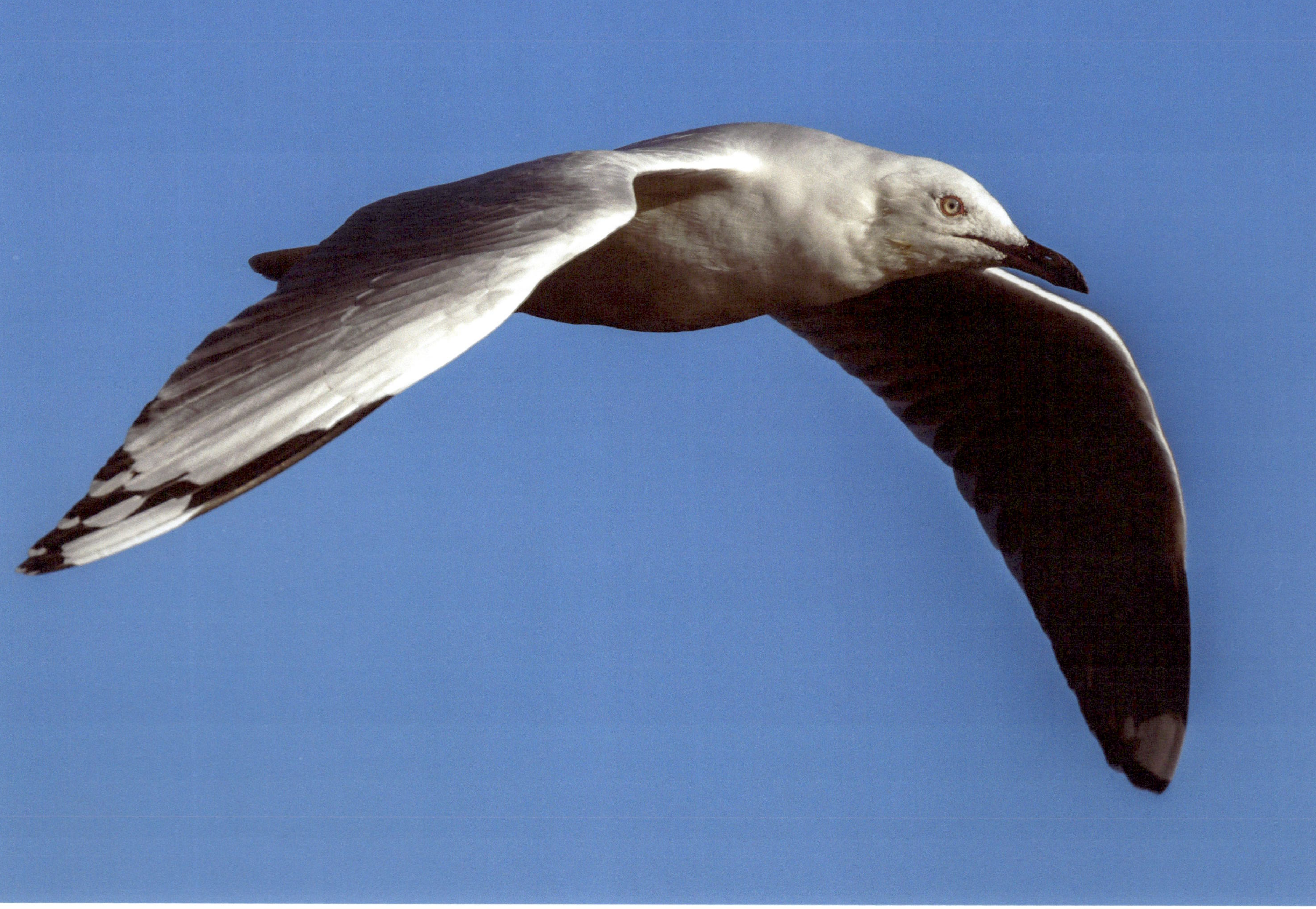

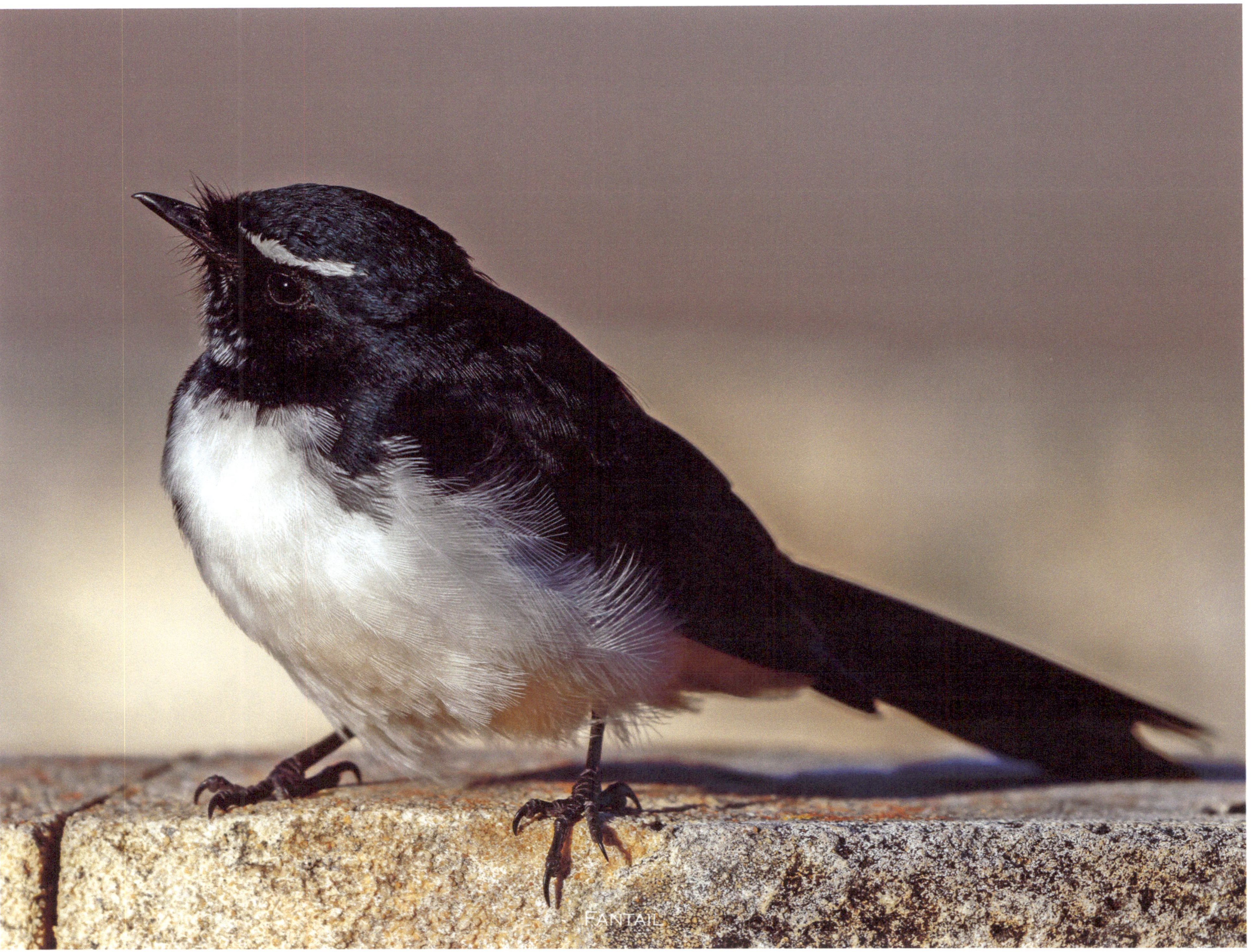

FANTAIL

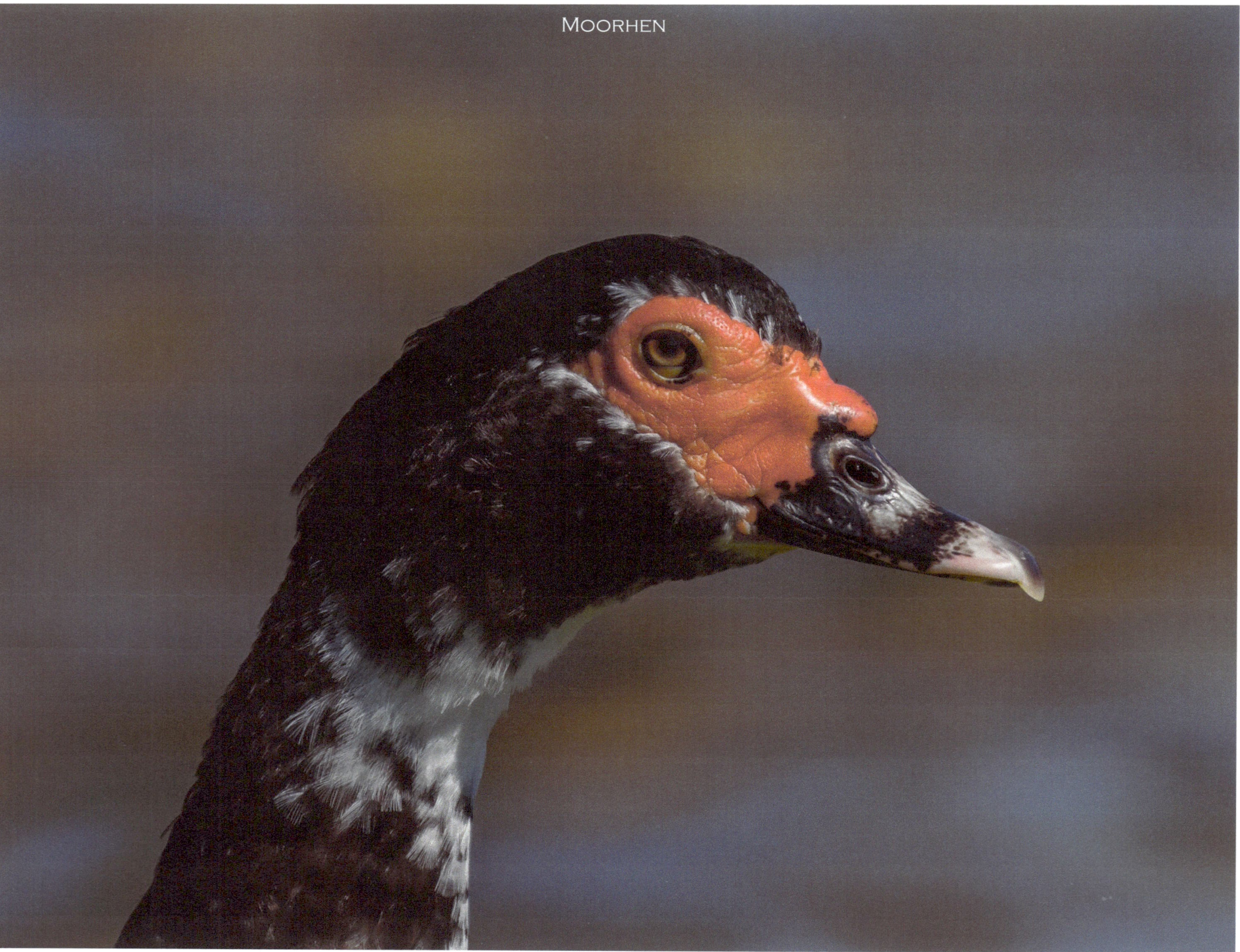

MOORHEN

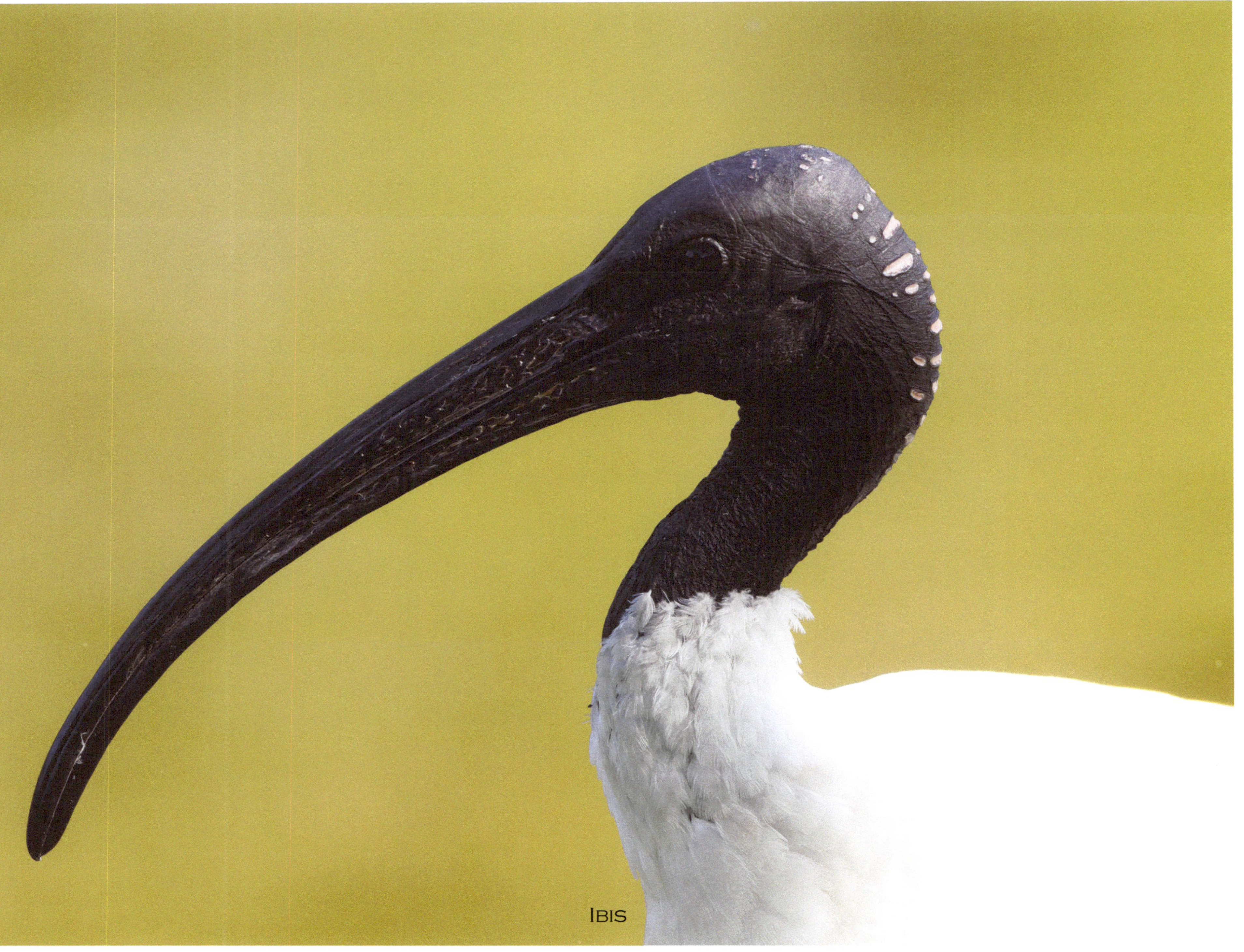

Ibis

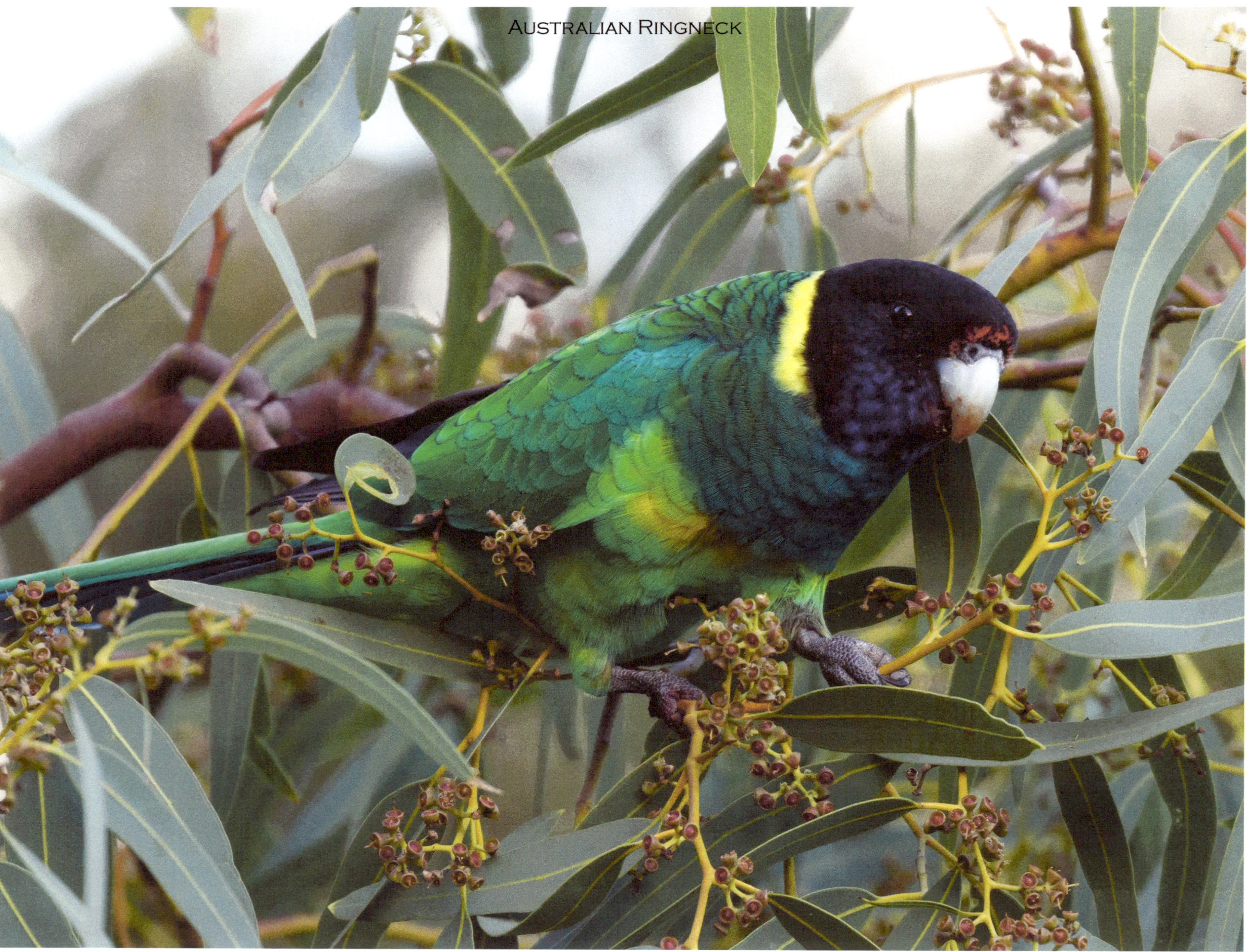

Australian Ringneck

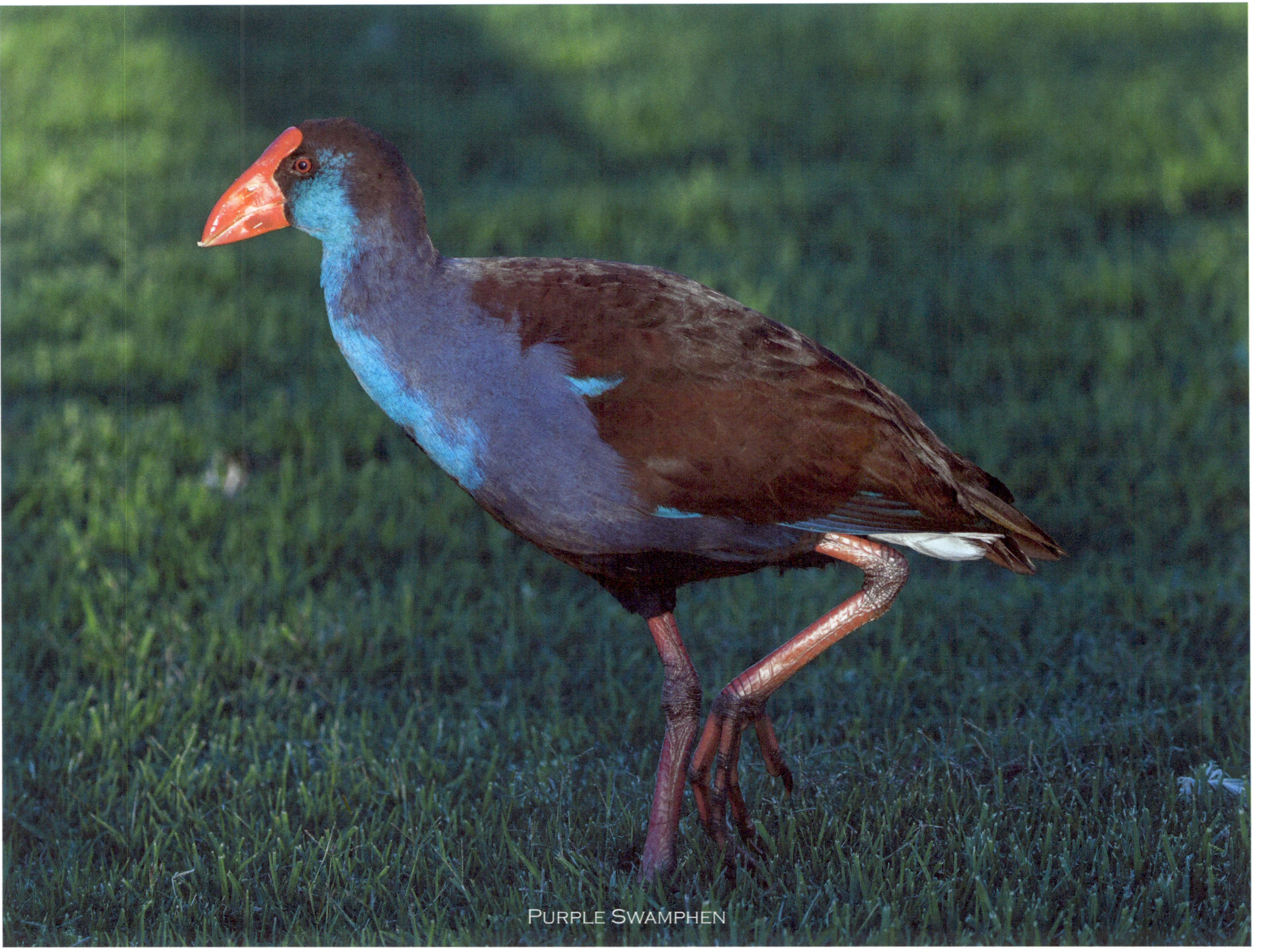

Purple Swamphen

Duck

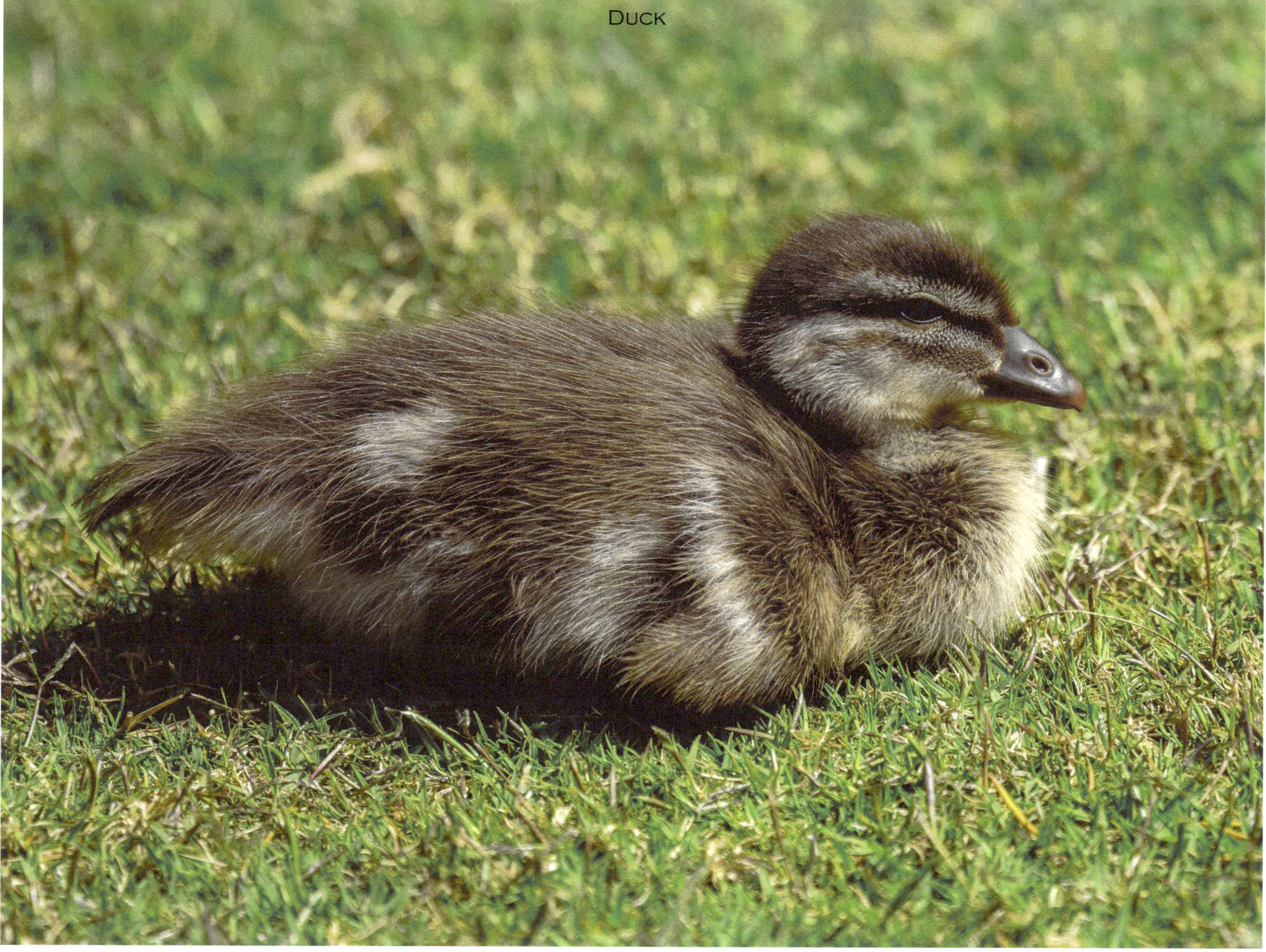

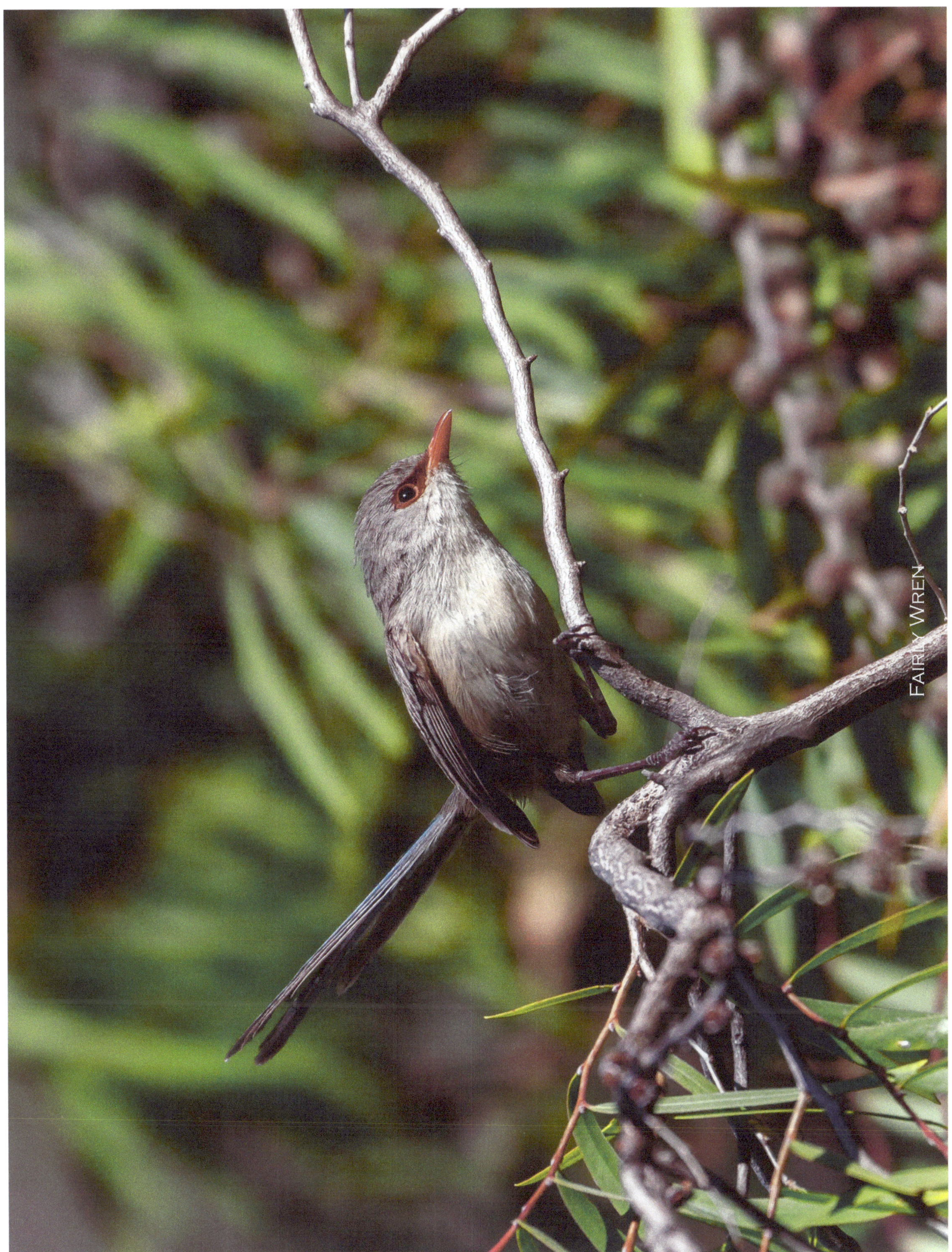
FAIRY WREN

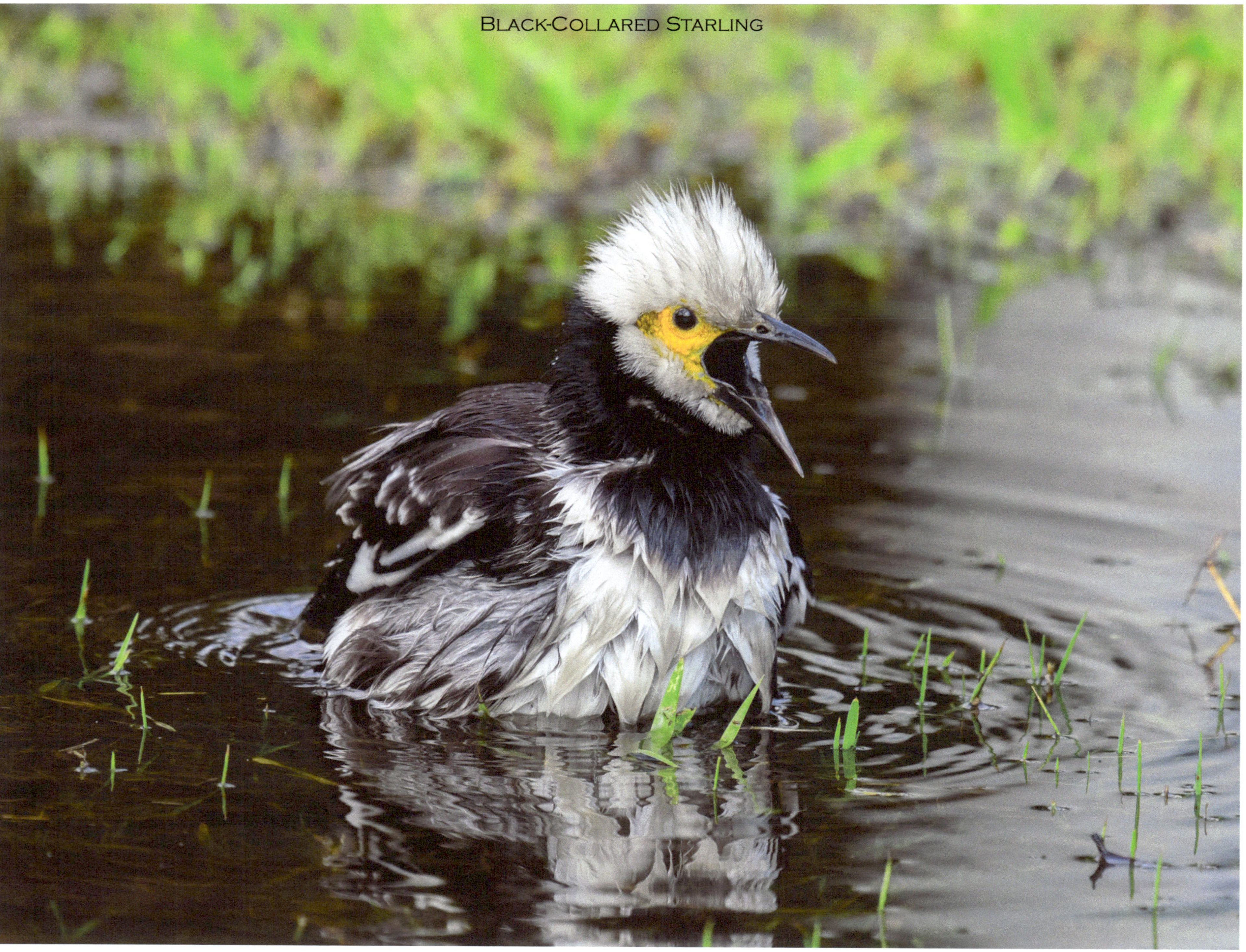

BLACK-COLLARED STARLING

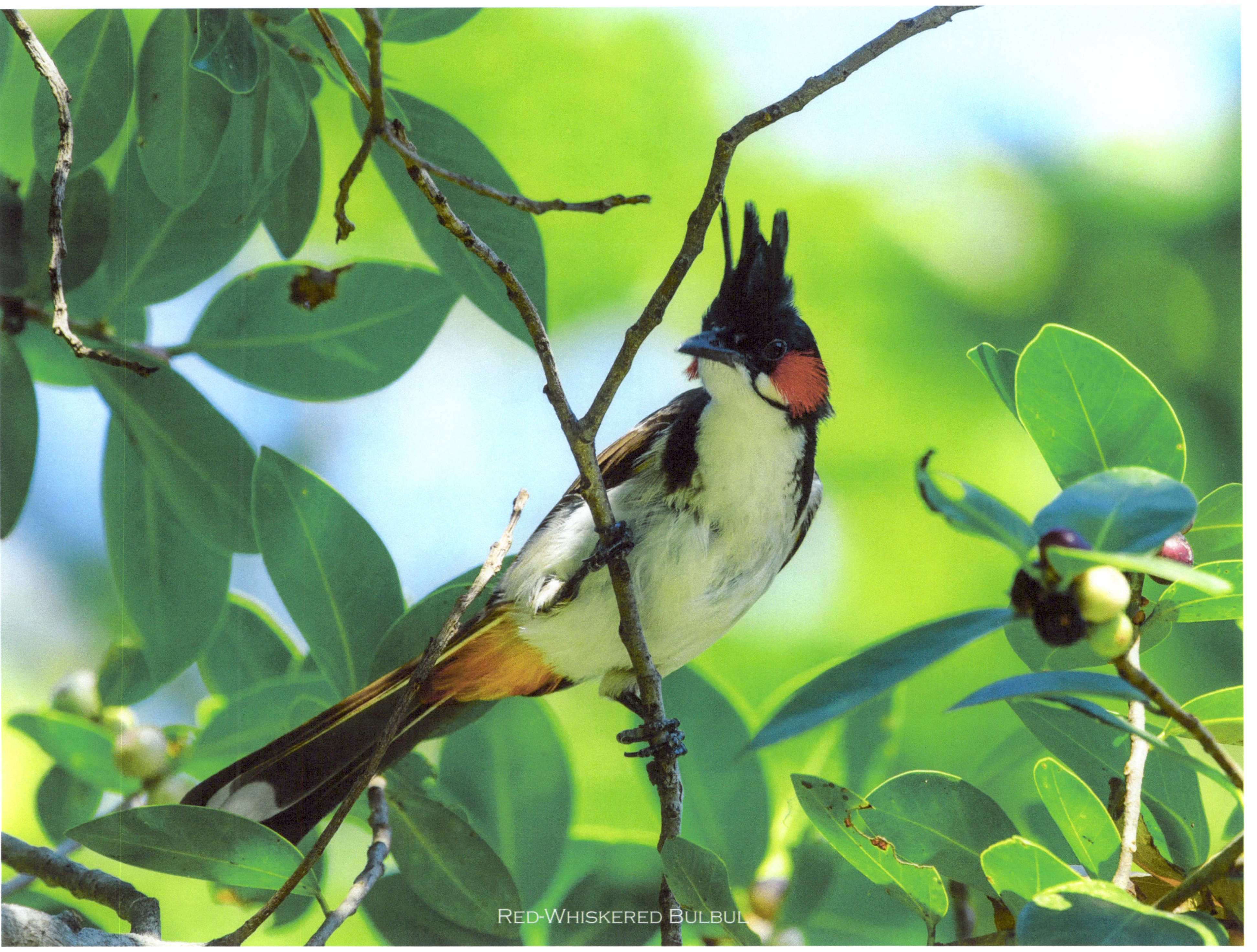
Red-Whiskered Bulbul

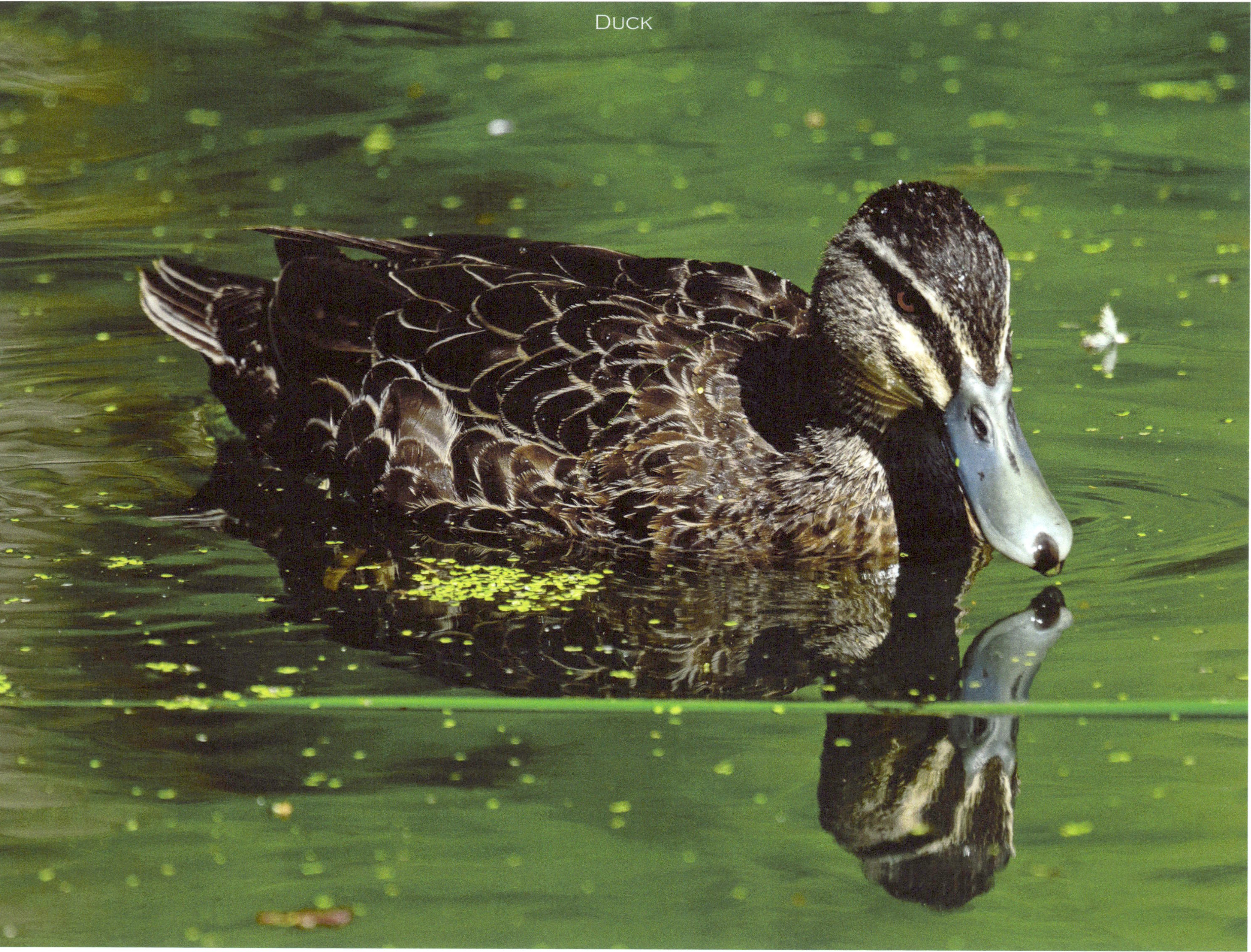

DUCK

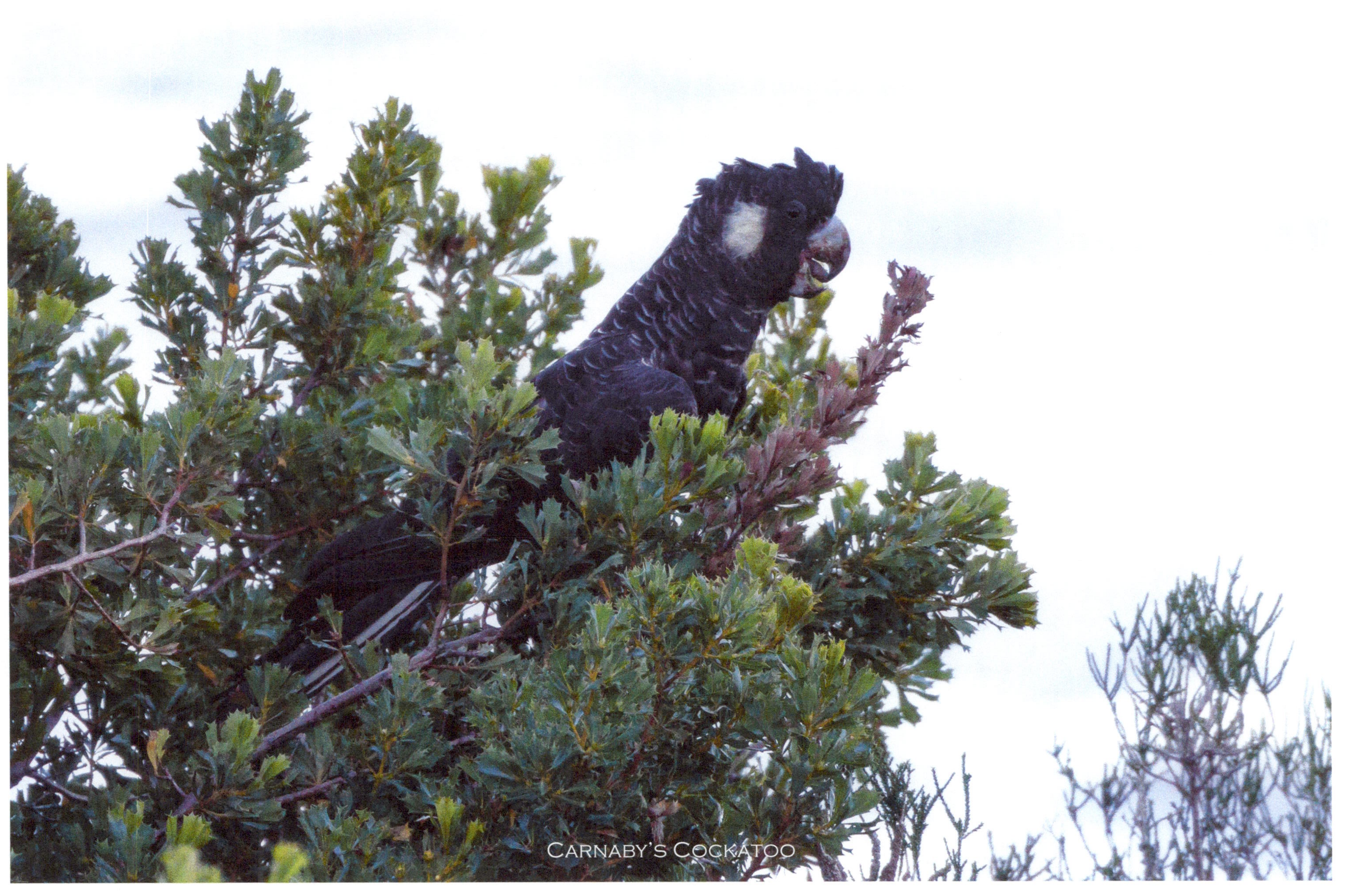

Carnaby's Cockatoo

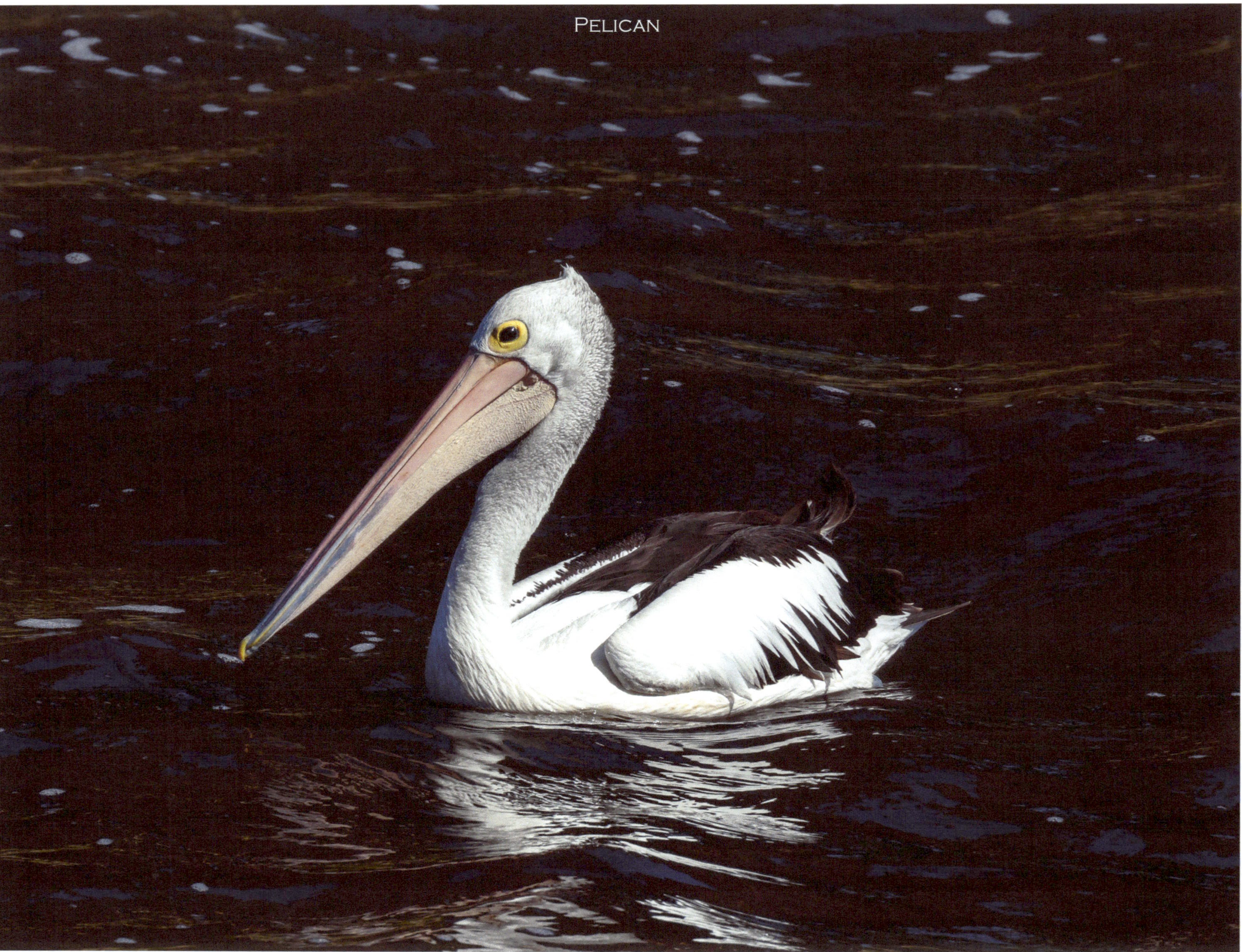

Pelican

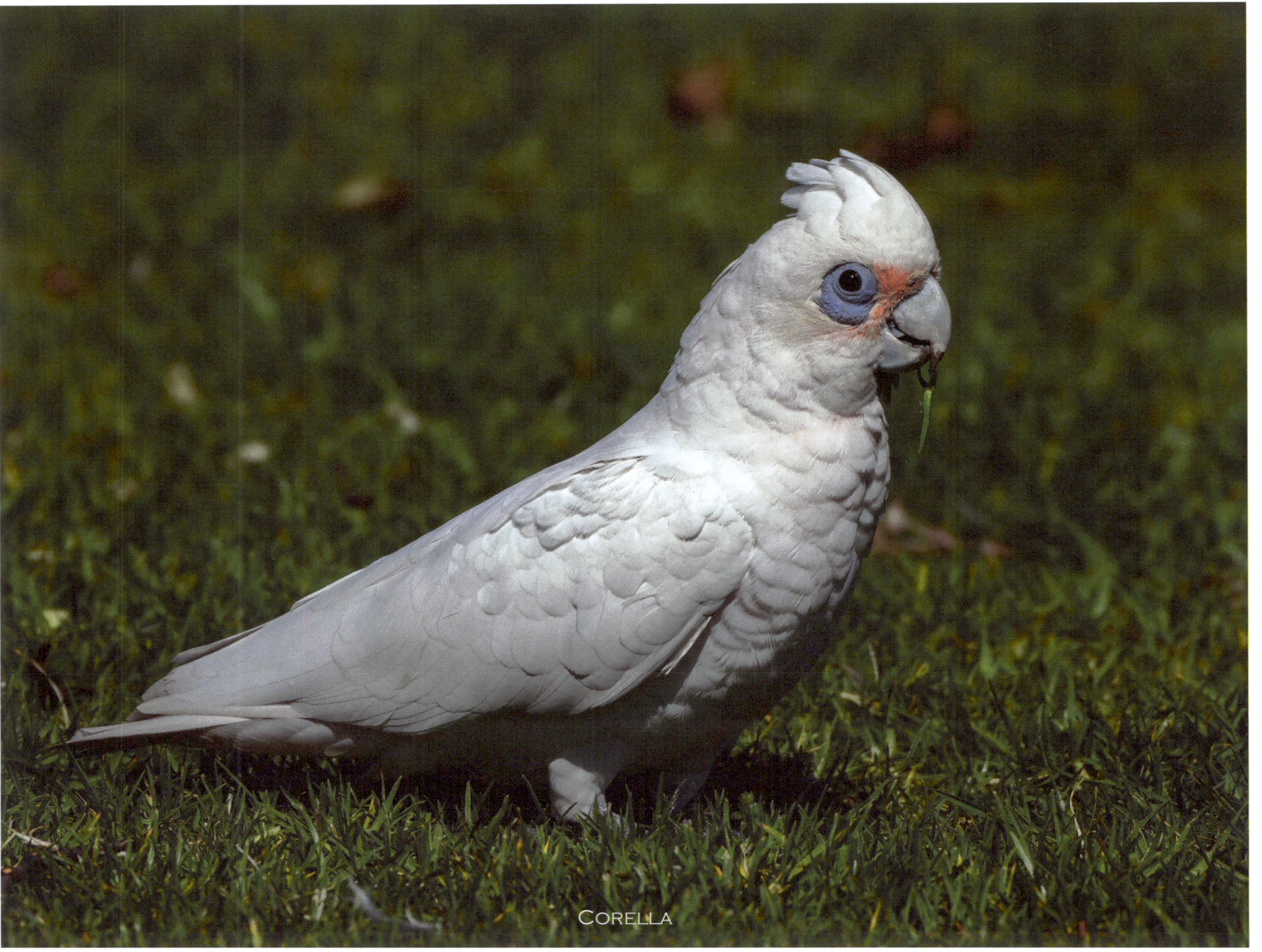

Corella

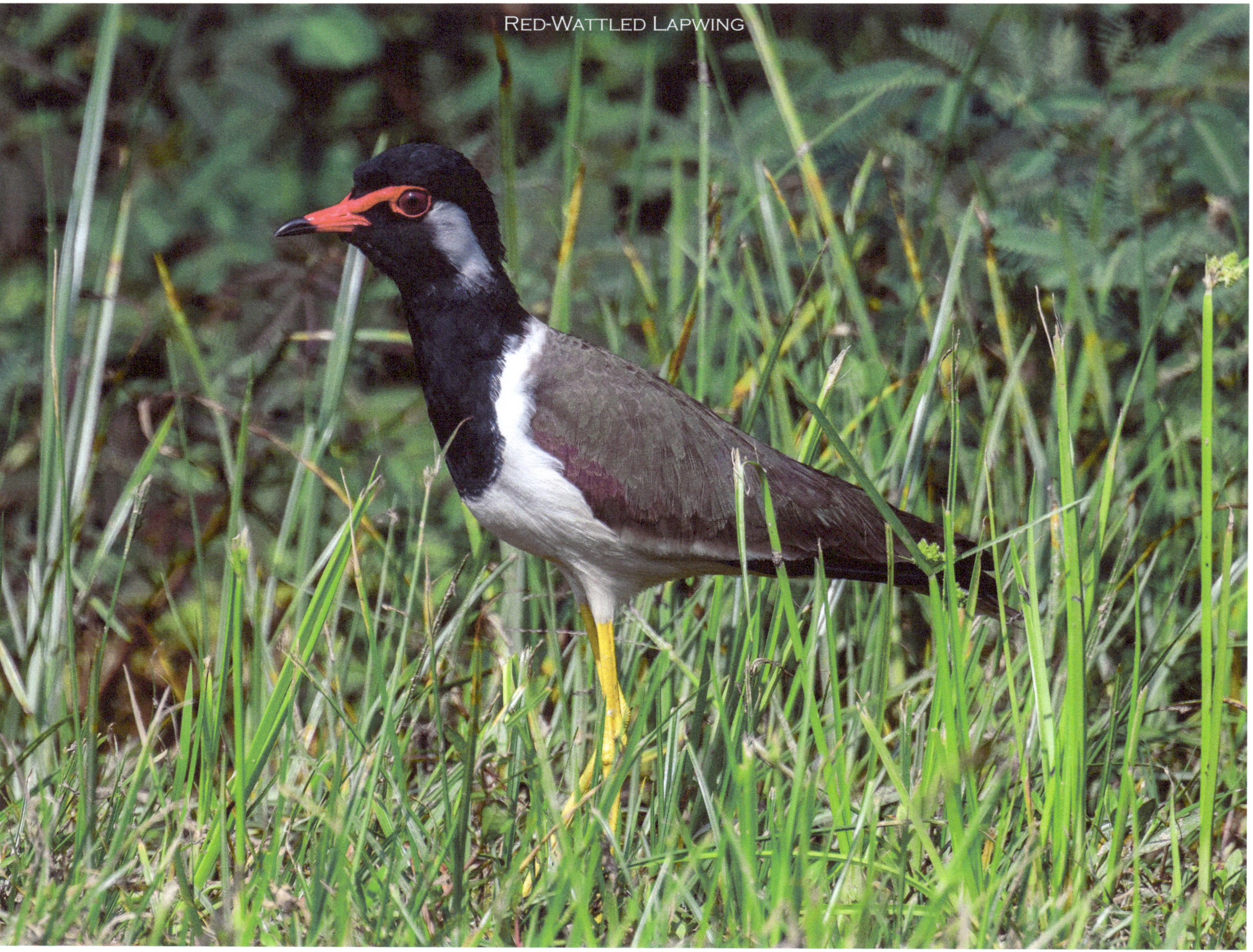

Red-Wattled Lapwing

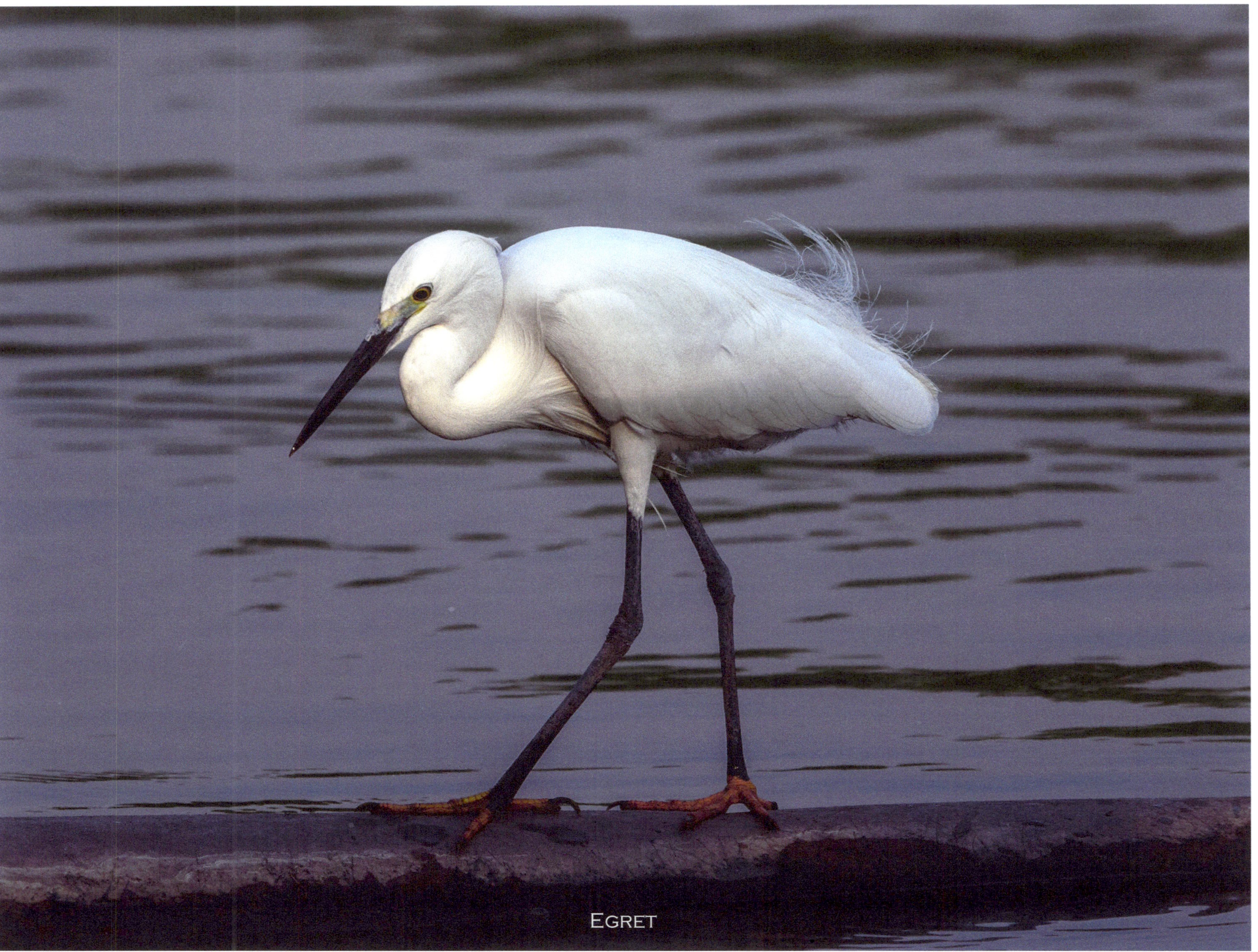

Egret

Wattlebird

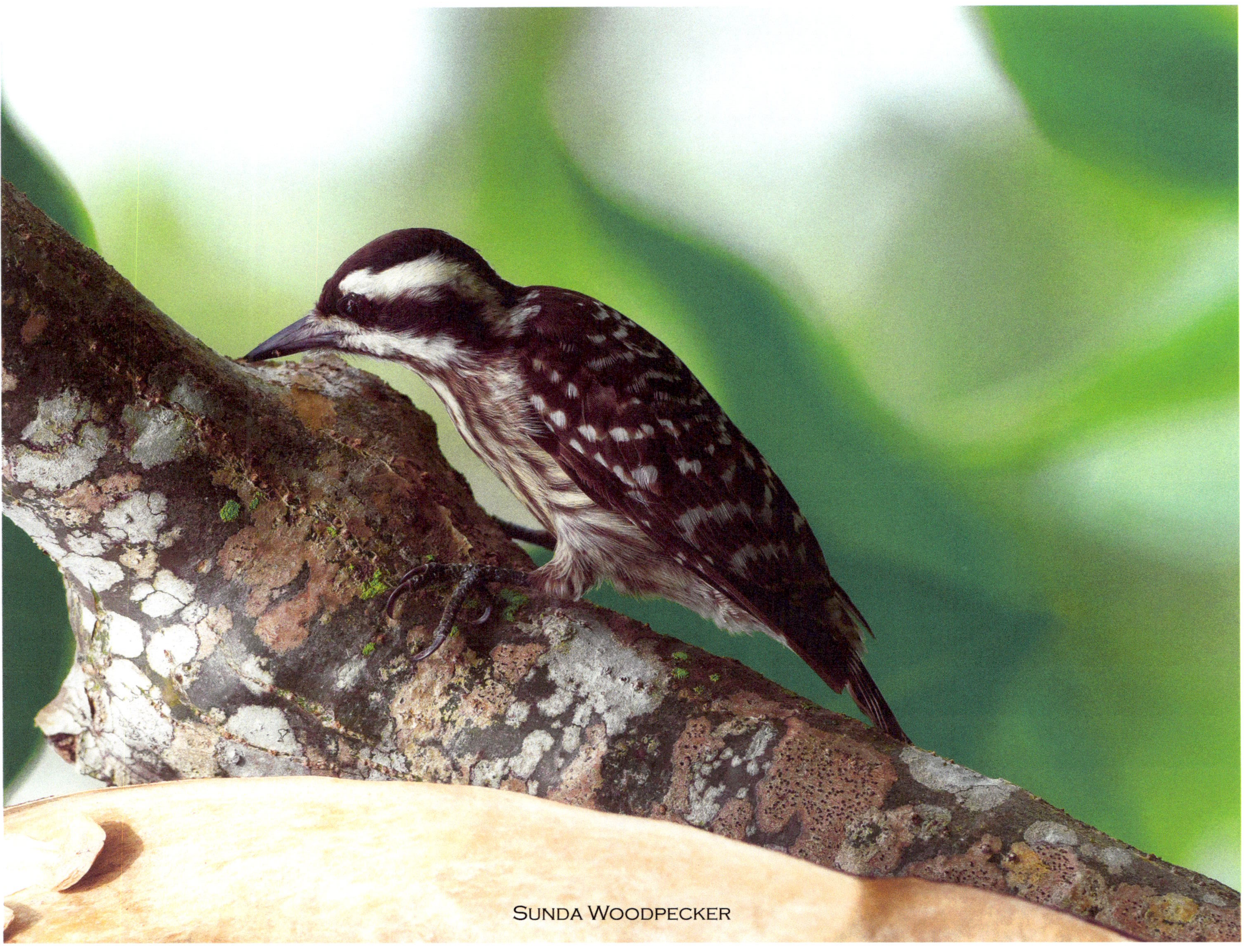

Sunda Woodpecker

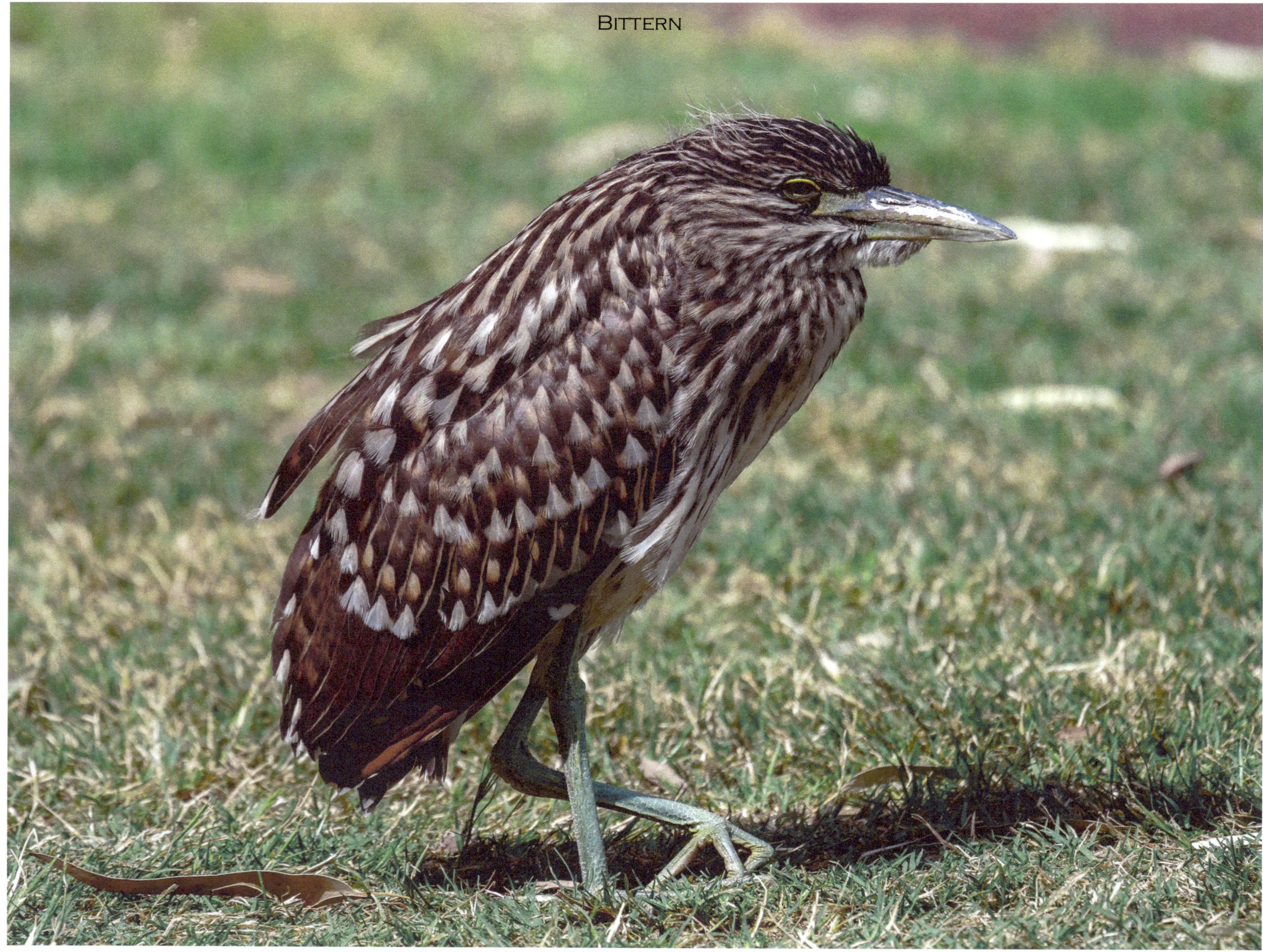

Bittern

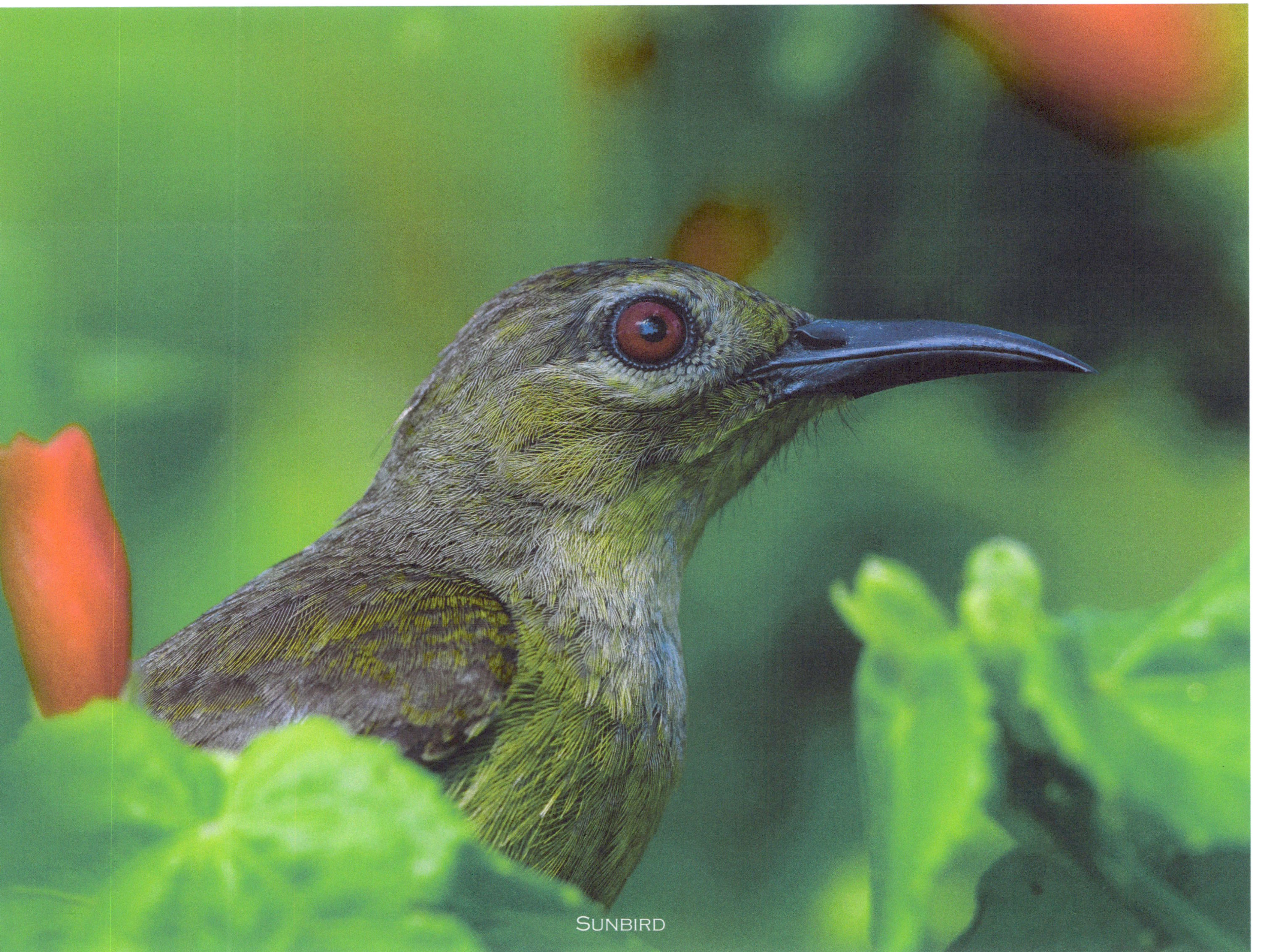

SUNBIRD

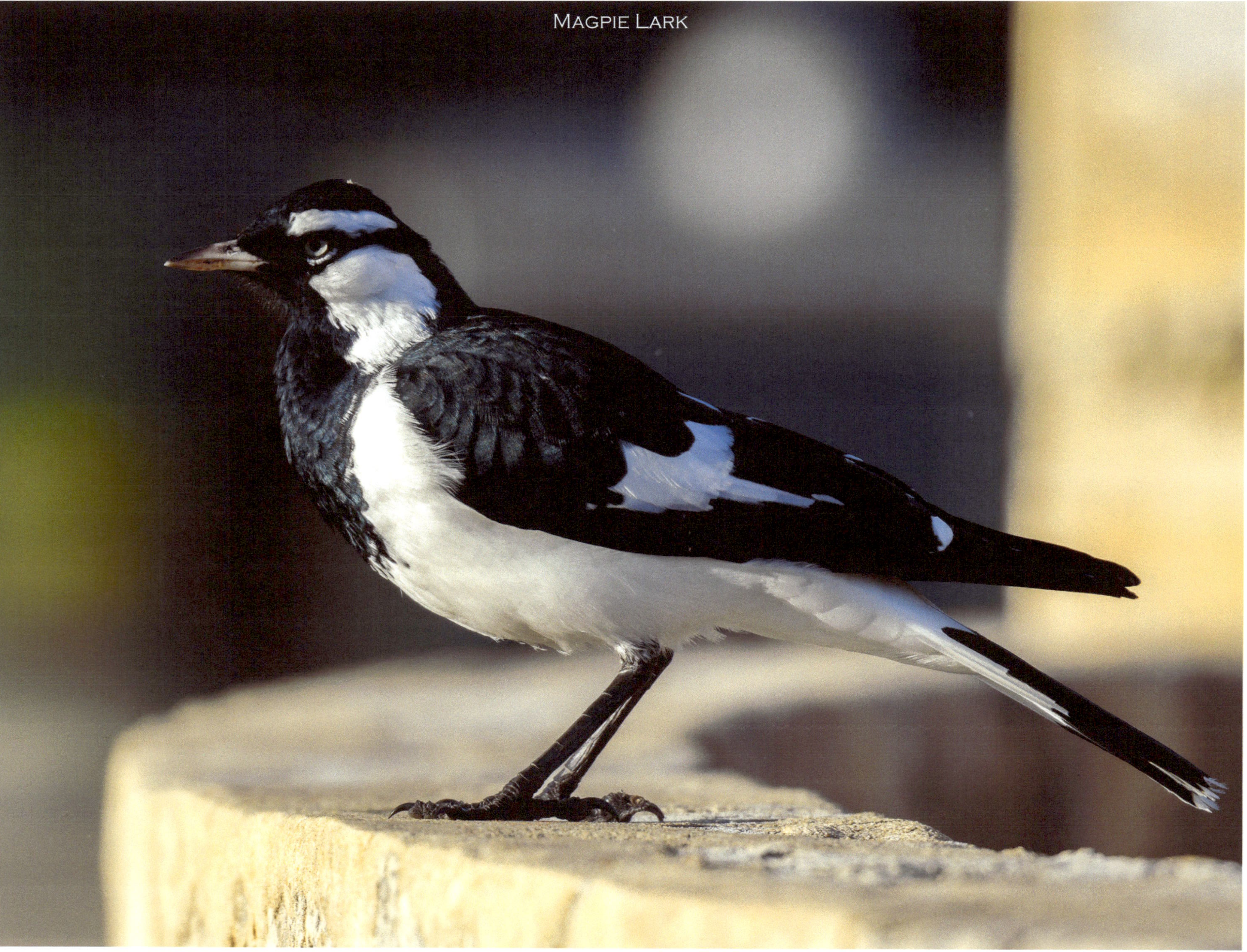

Magpie Lark

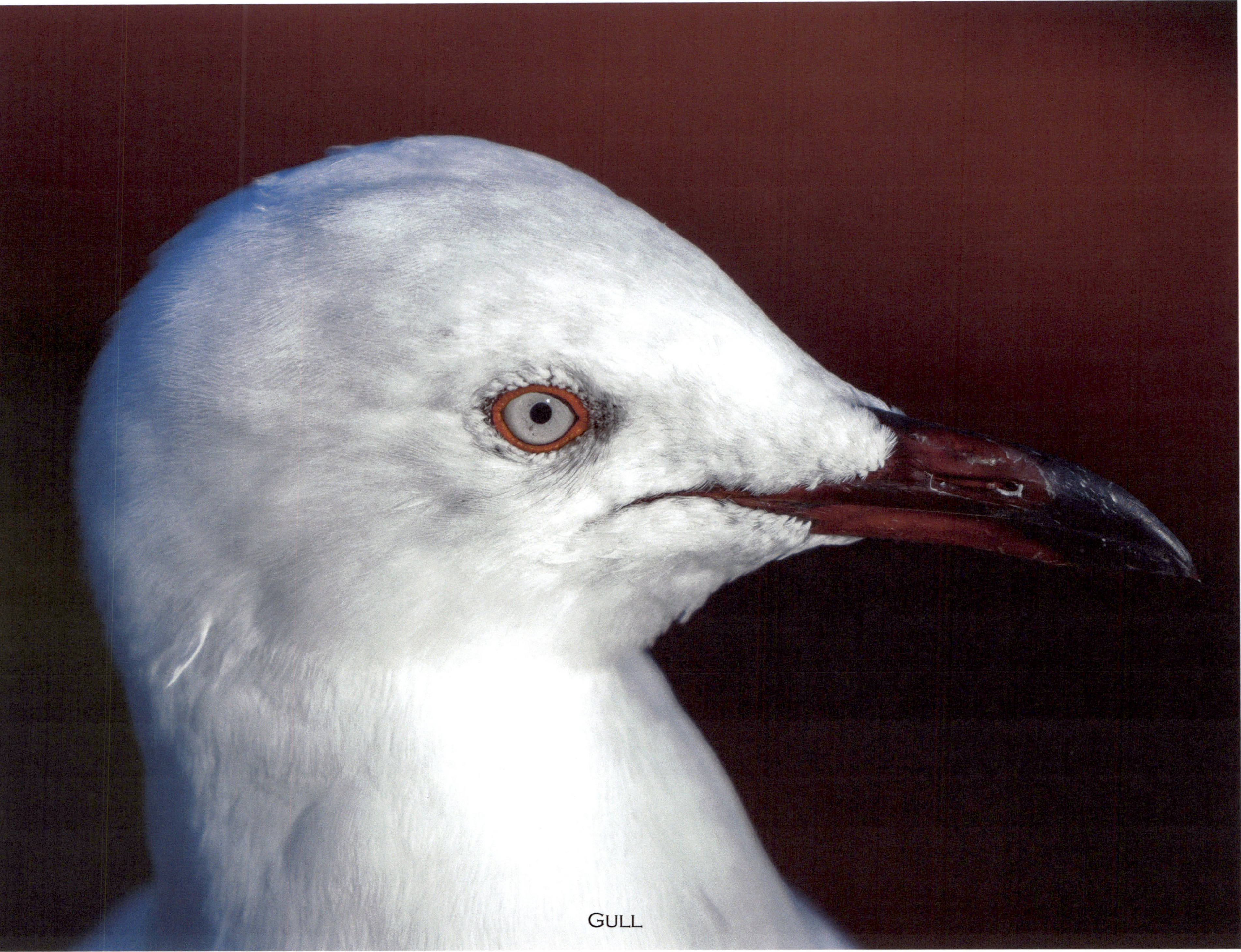

Gull

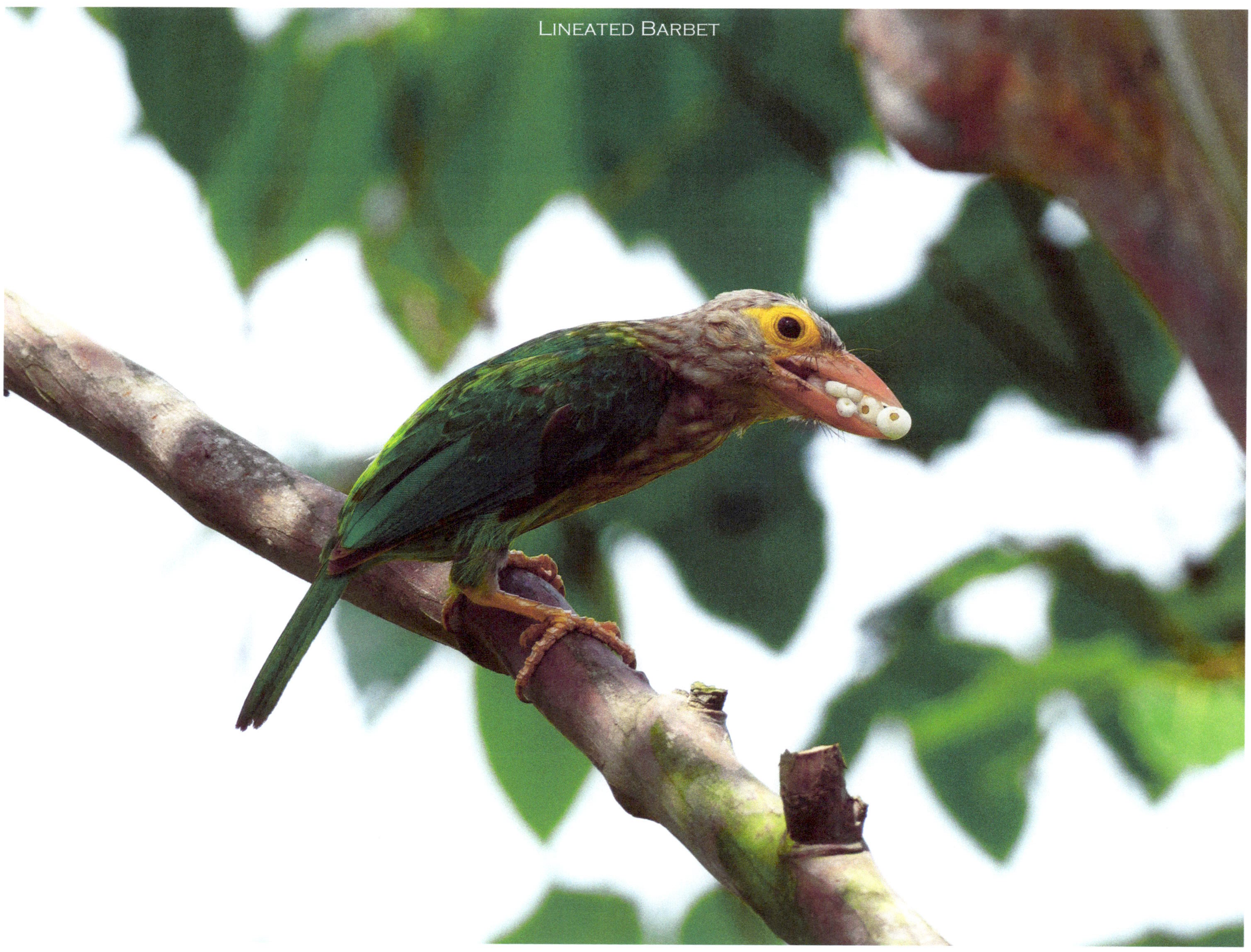

Lineated Barbet

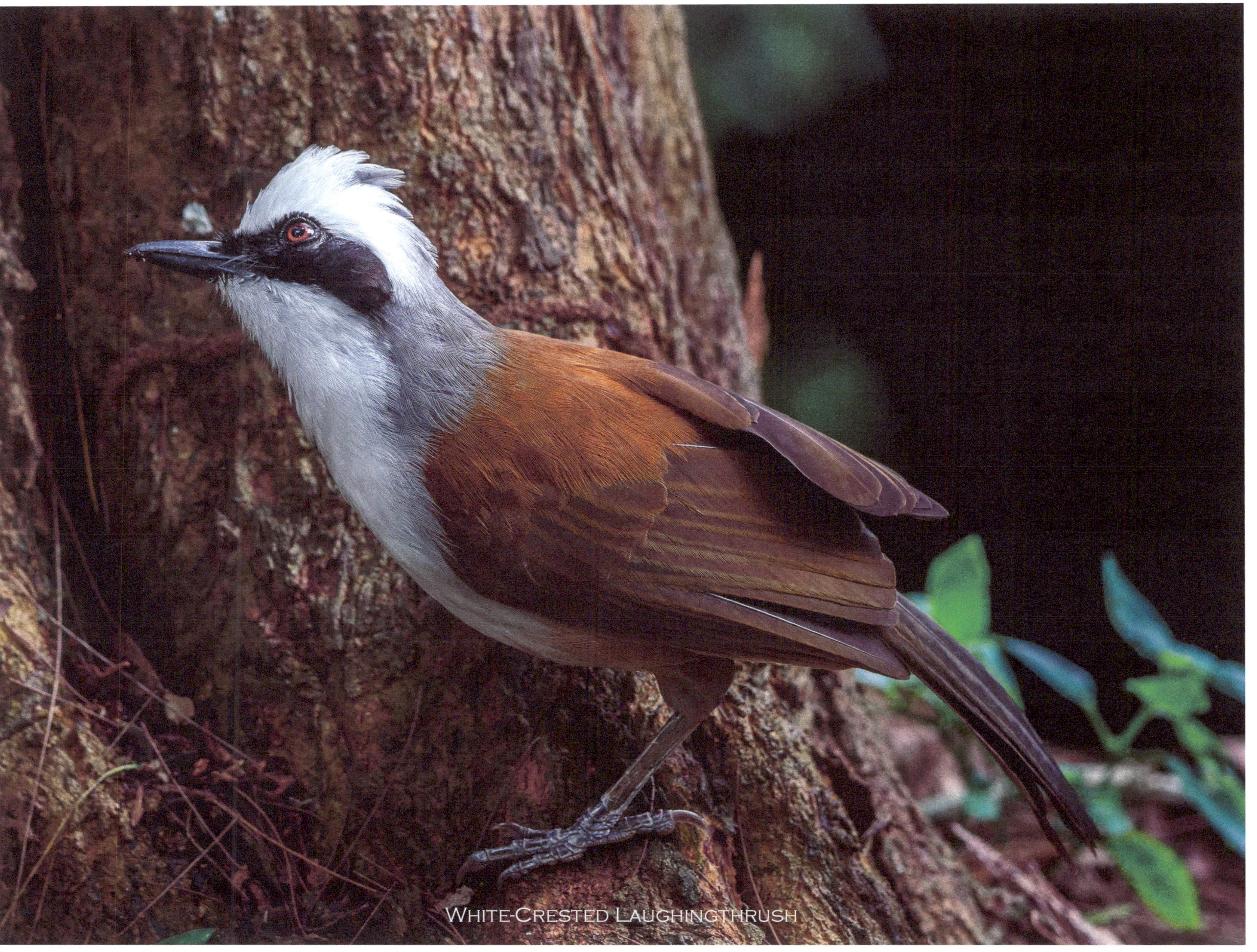

WHITE-CRESTED LAUGHINGTHRUSH

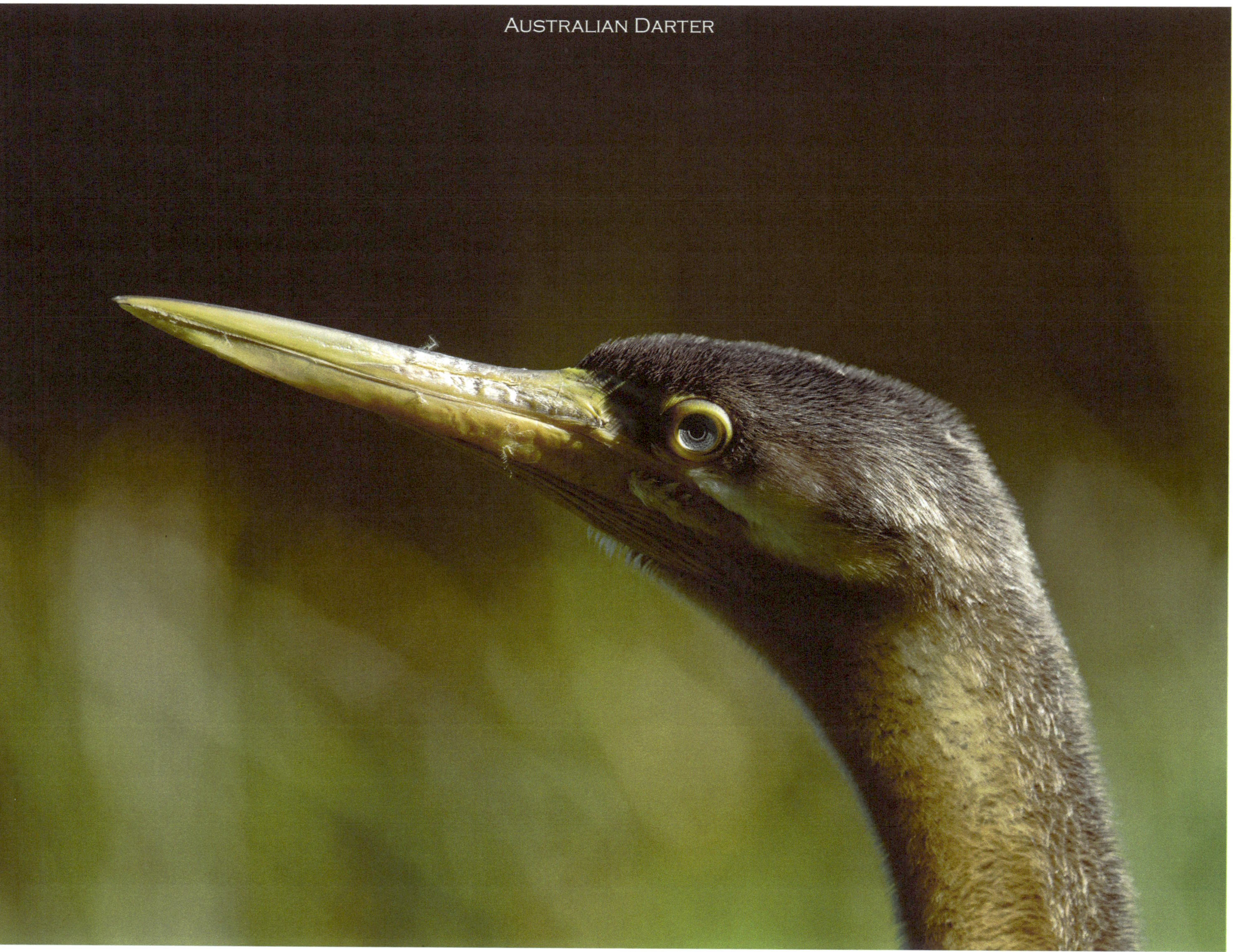

Australian Darter

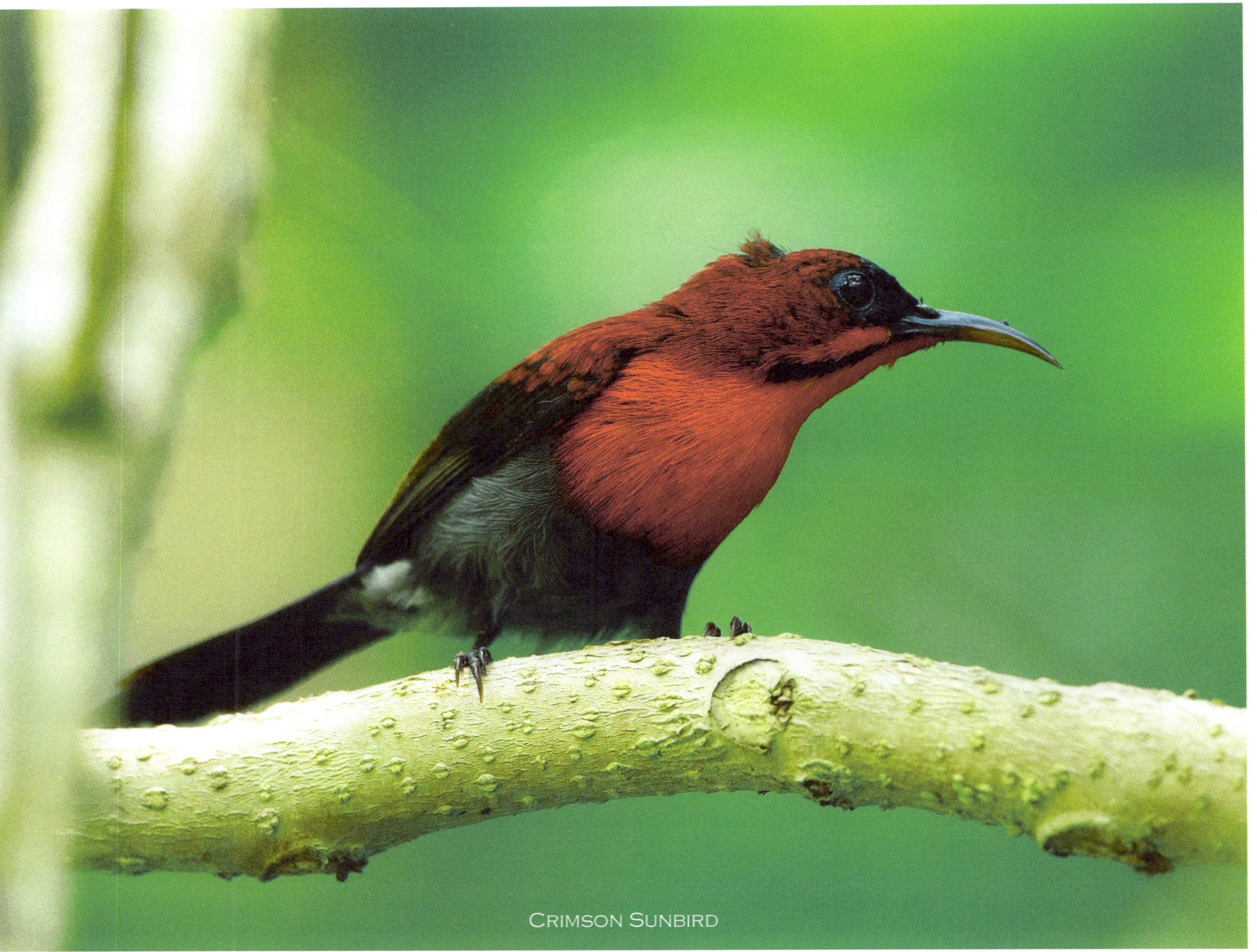

Crimson Sunbird

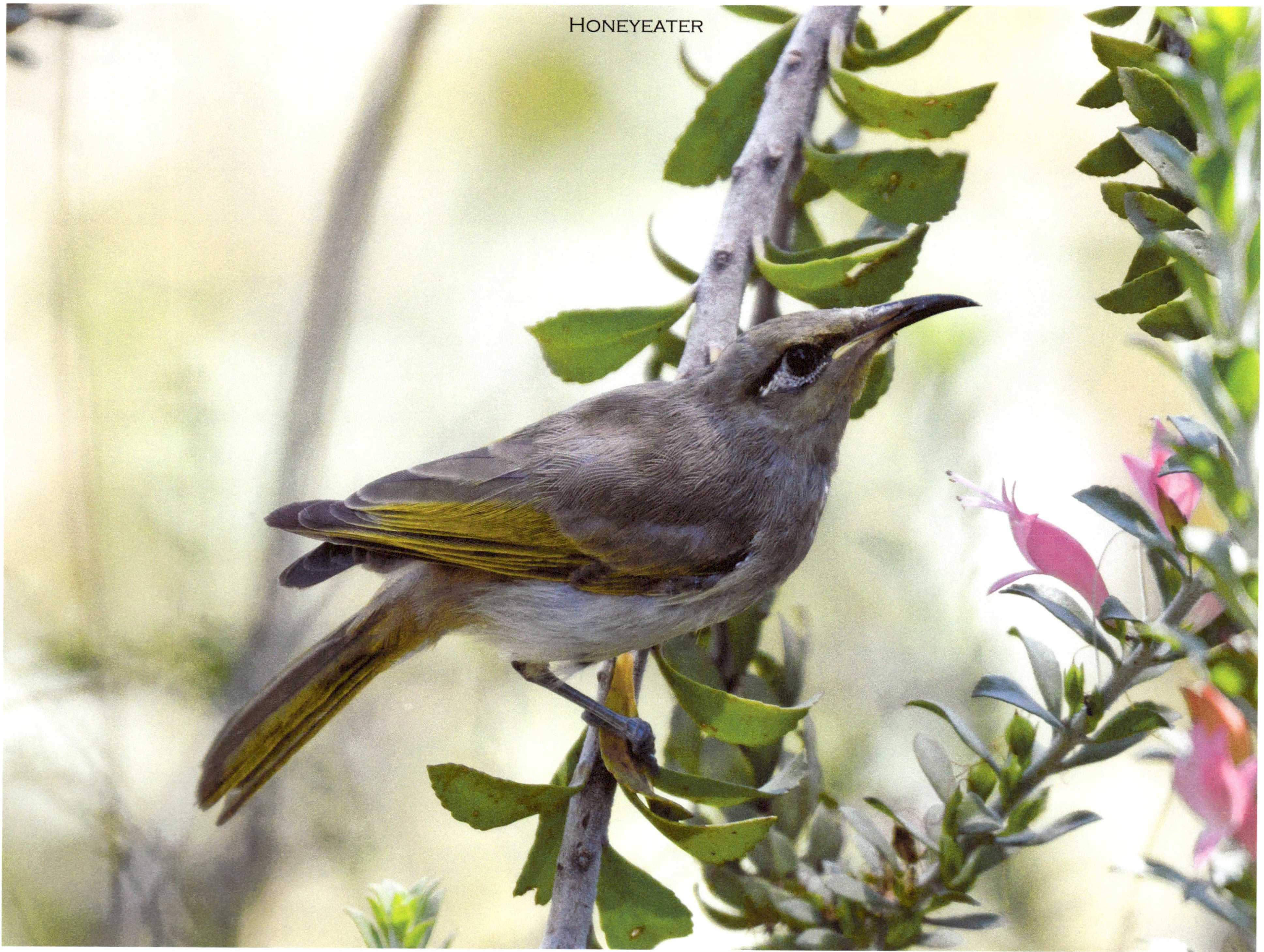

Honeyeater

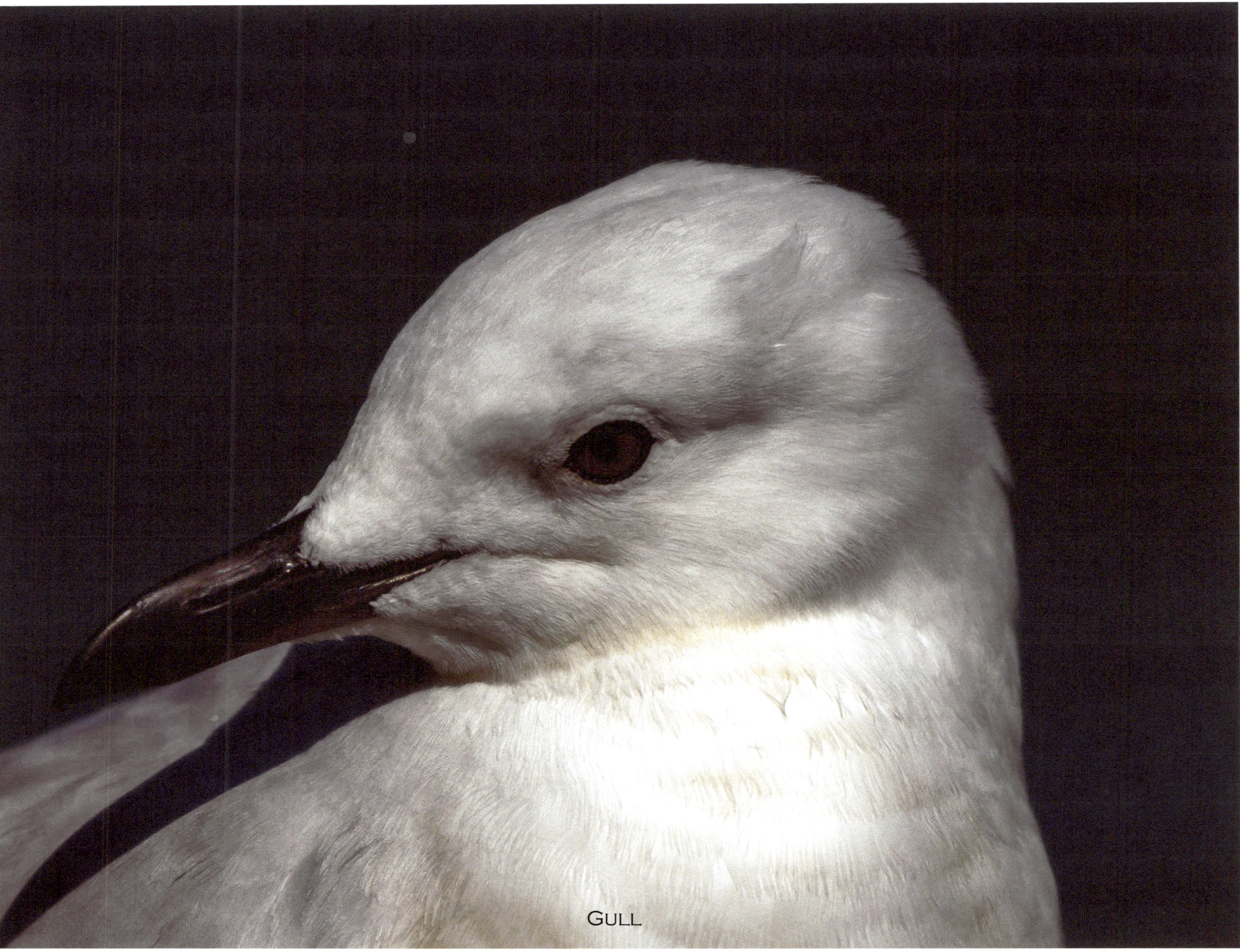

GULL

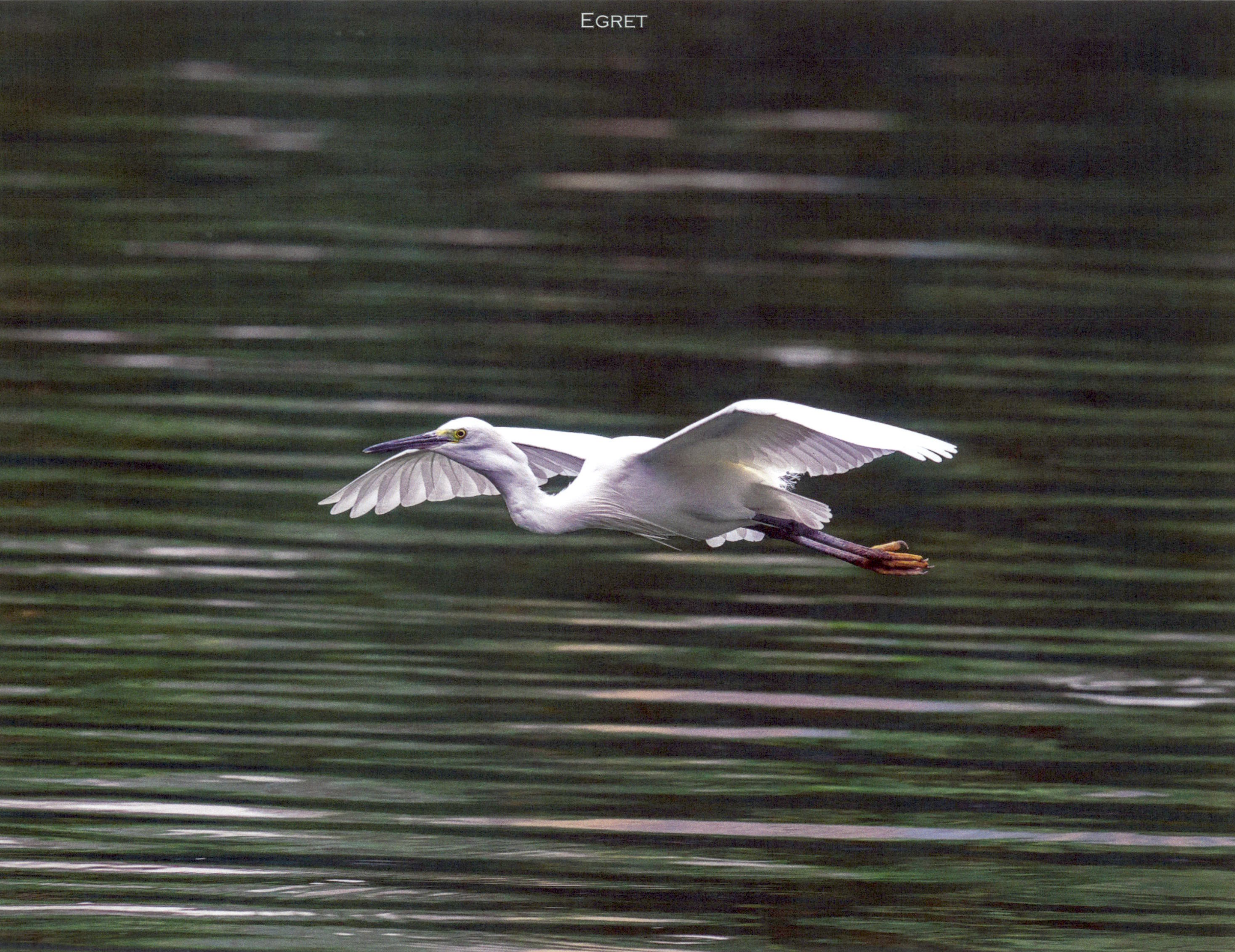

Egret

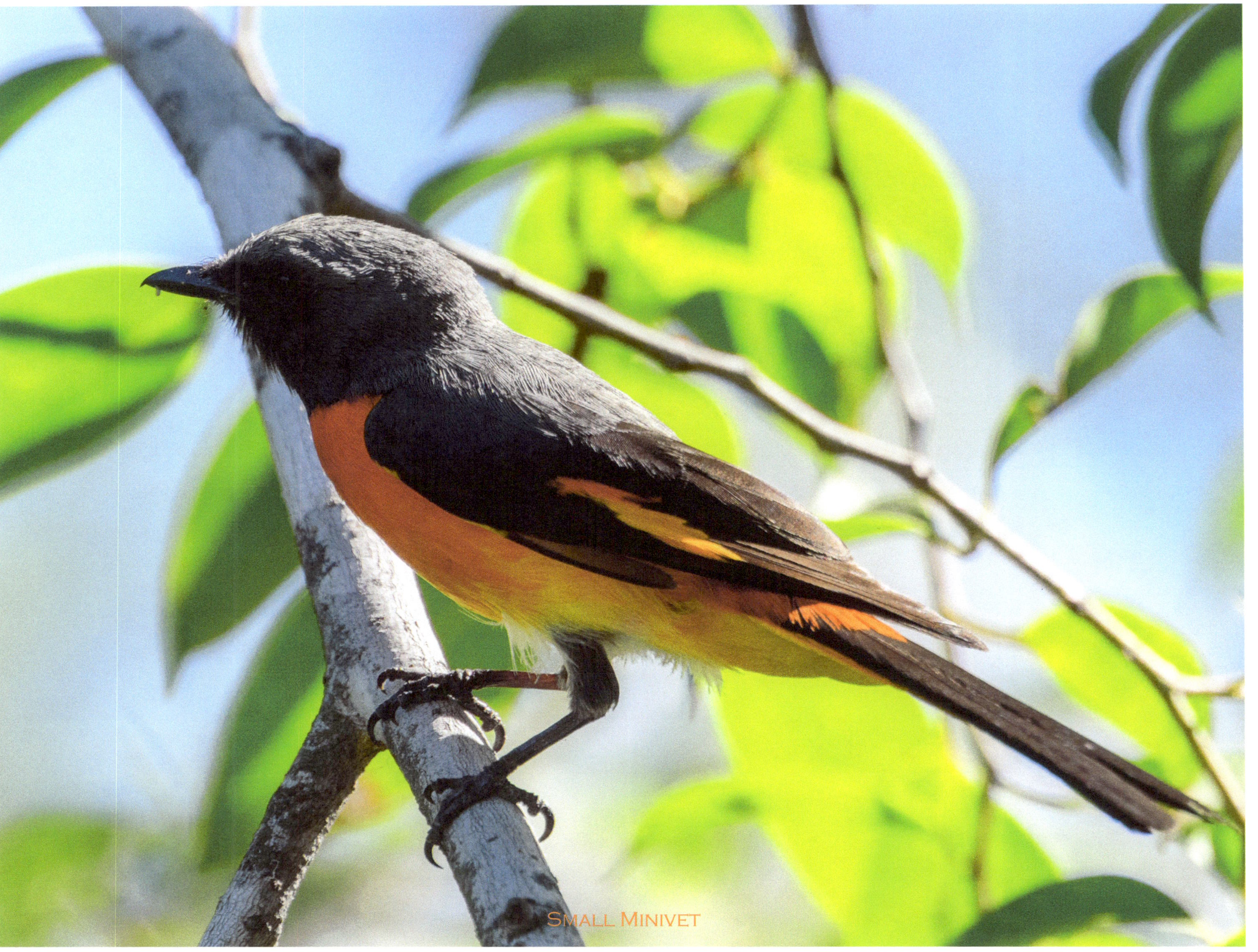

Small Minivet

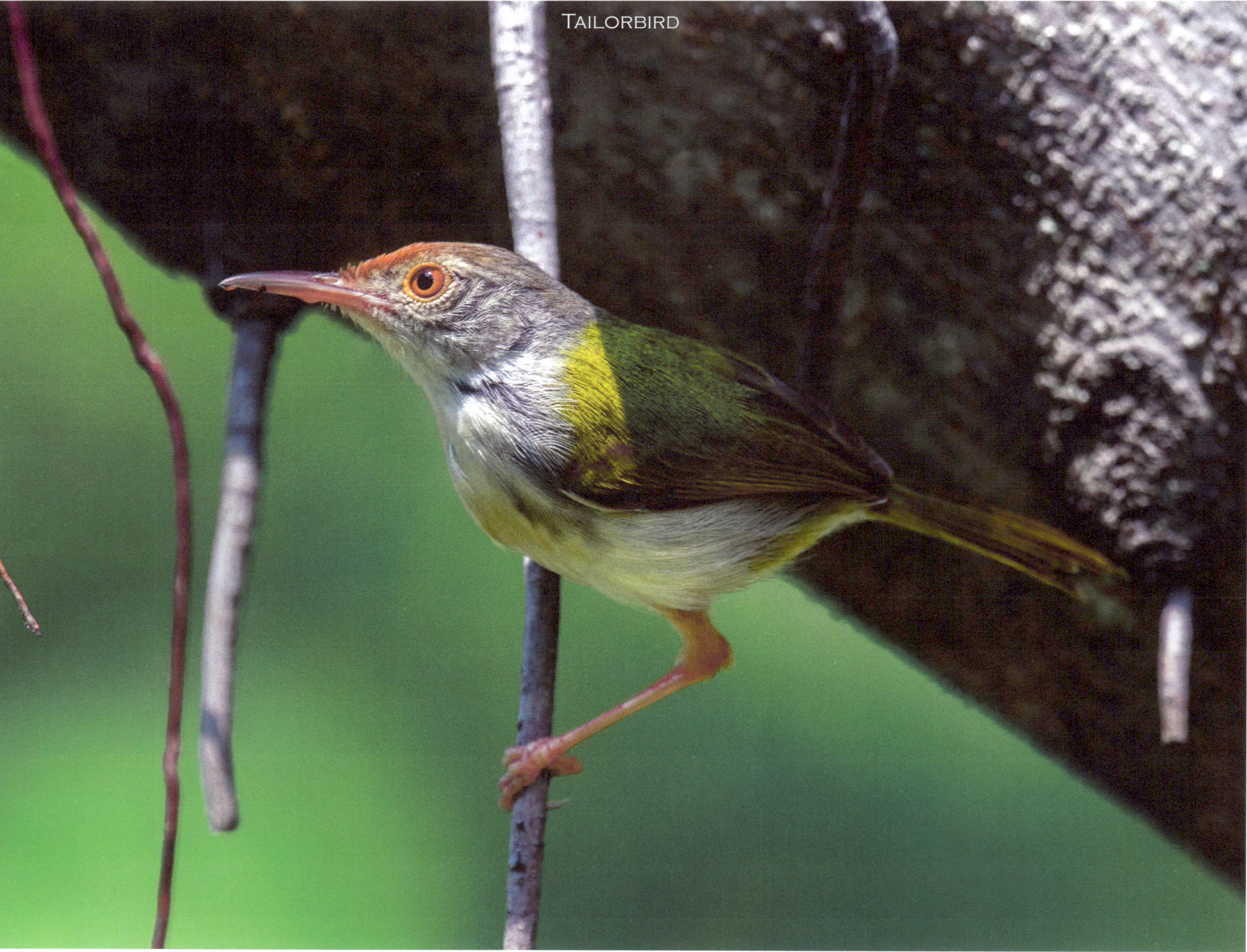

Tailorbird

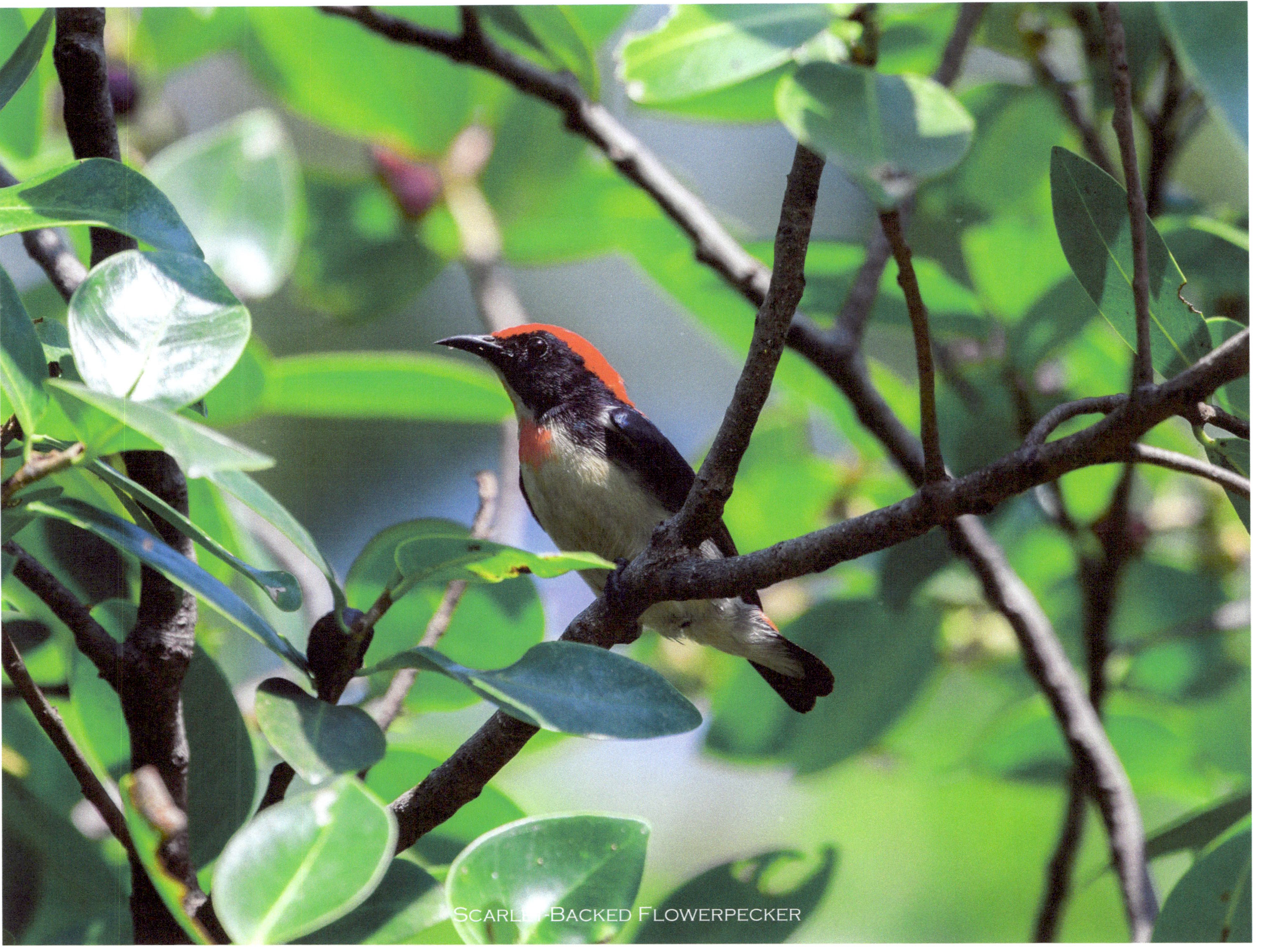

Scarlet-Backed Flowerpecker

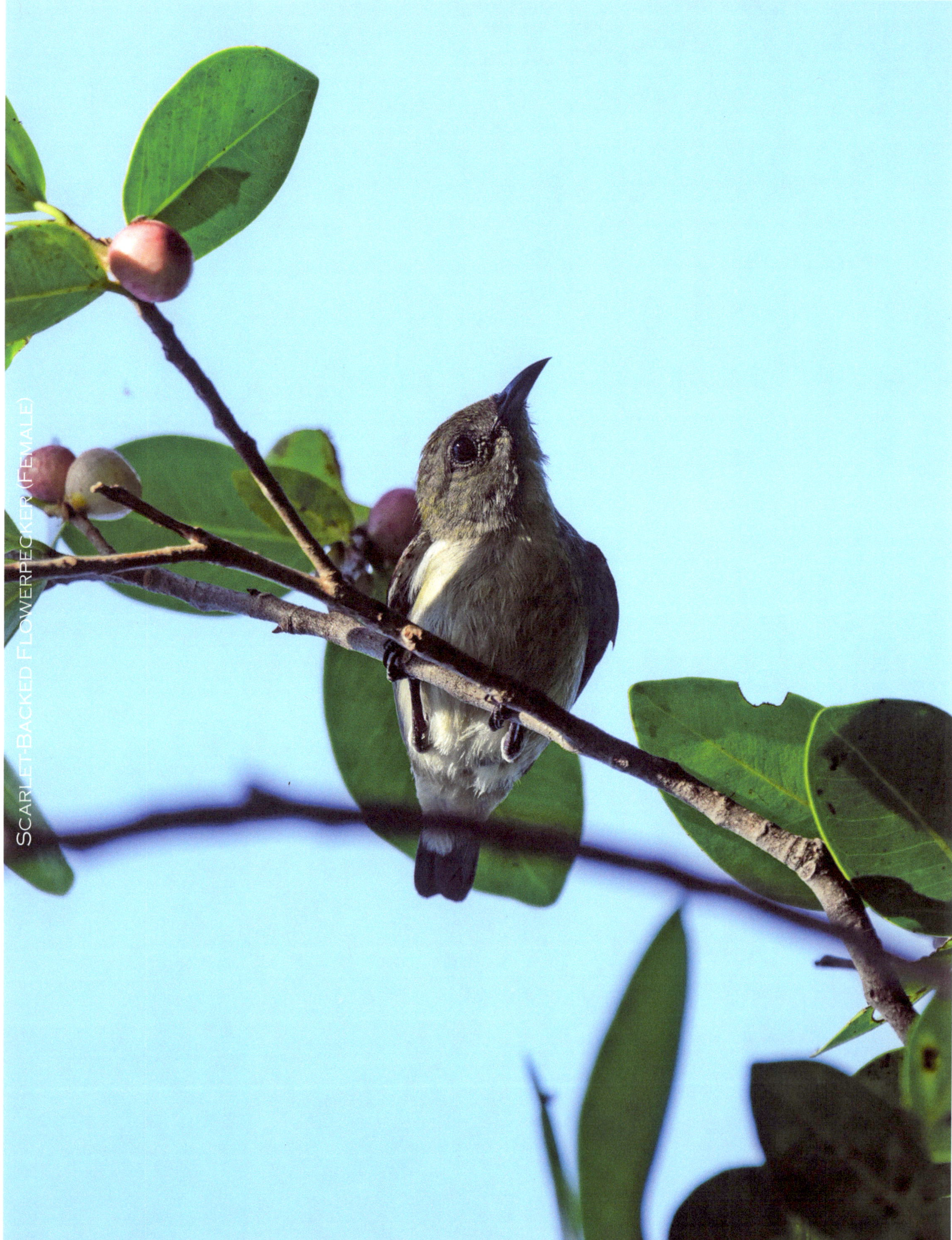

Scarlet-Backed Flowerpecker (Female)

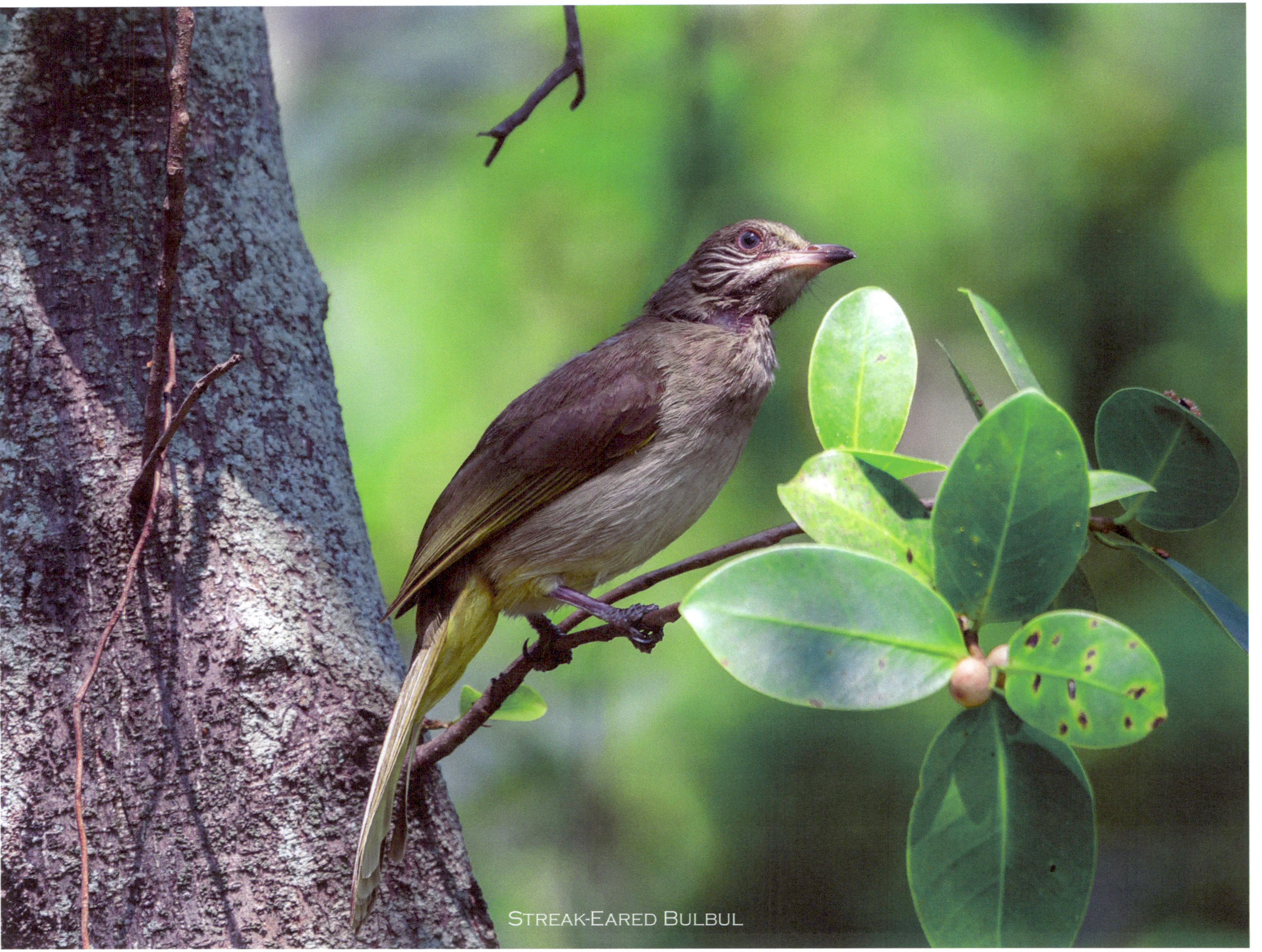
Streak-Eared Bulbul

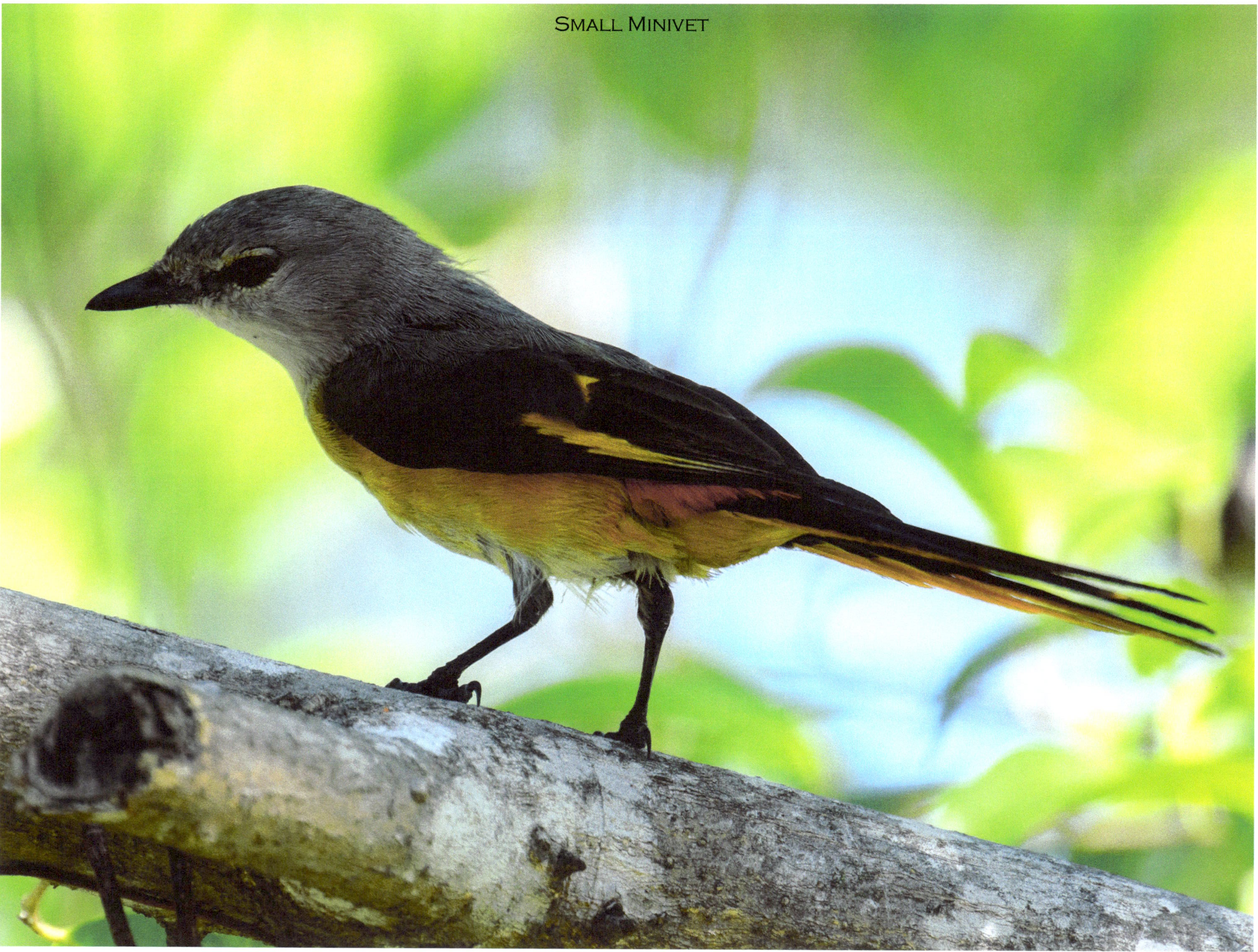

Small Minivet

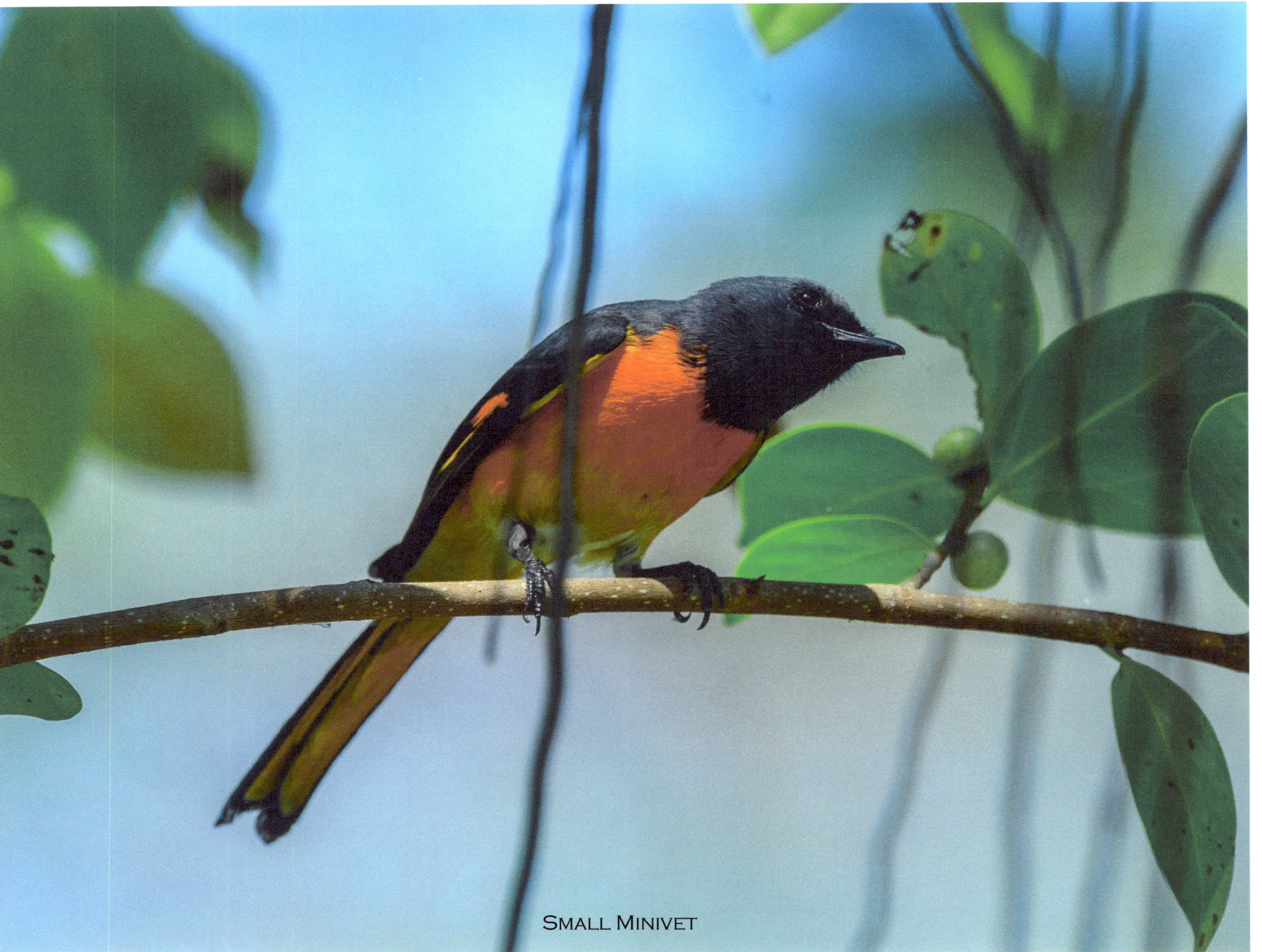

Small Minivet

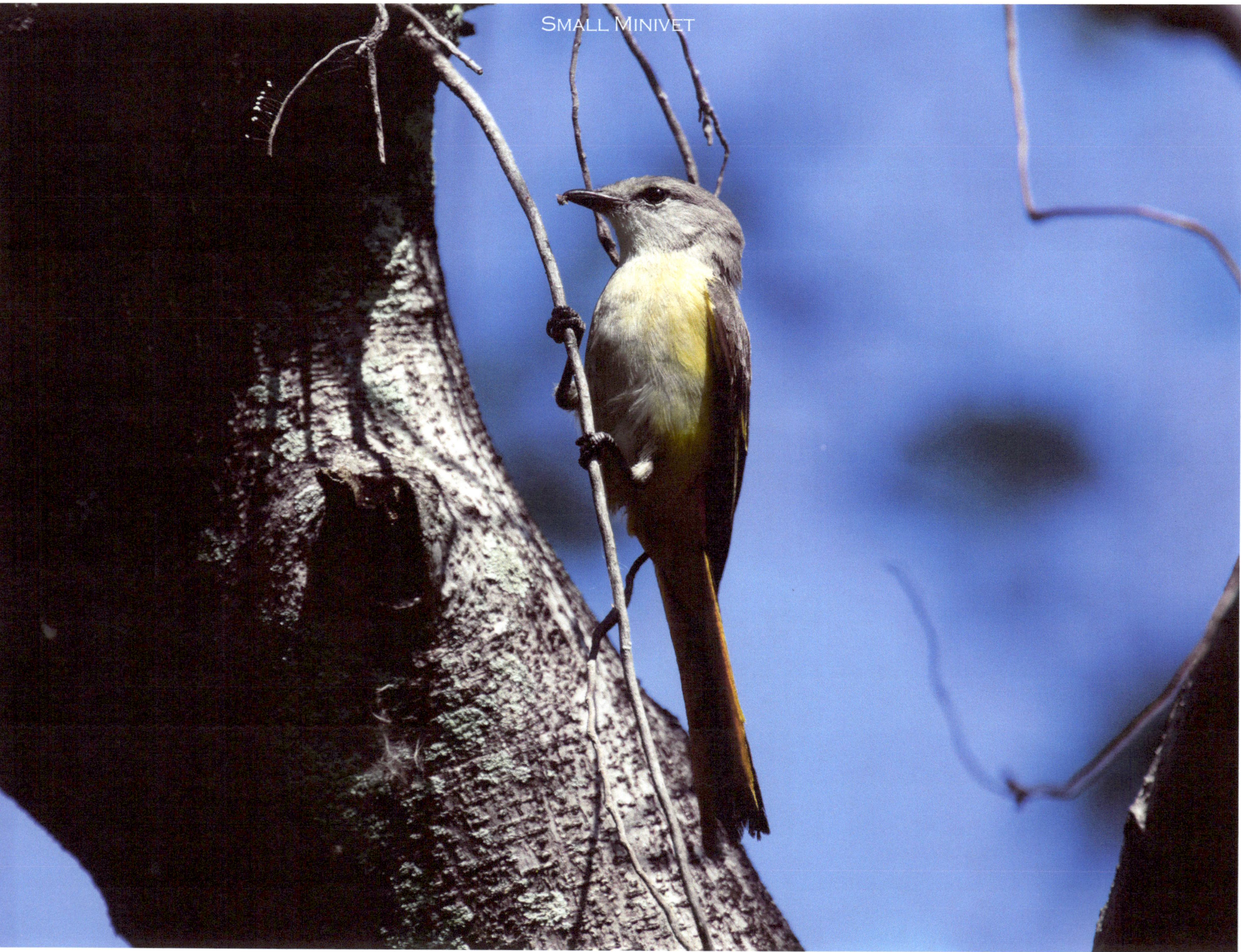

Small Minivet

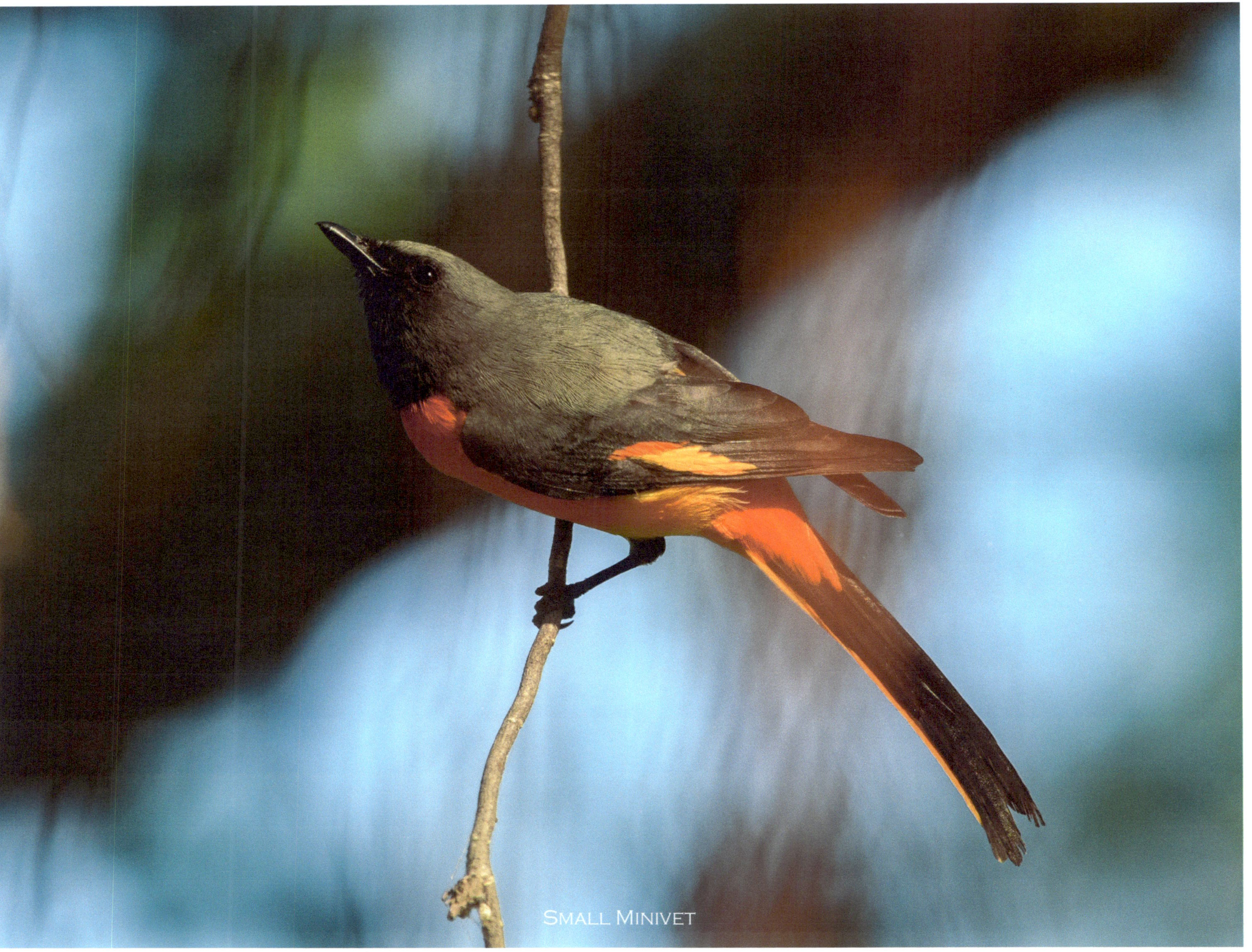

Small Minivet

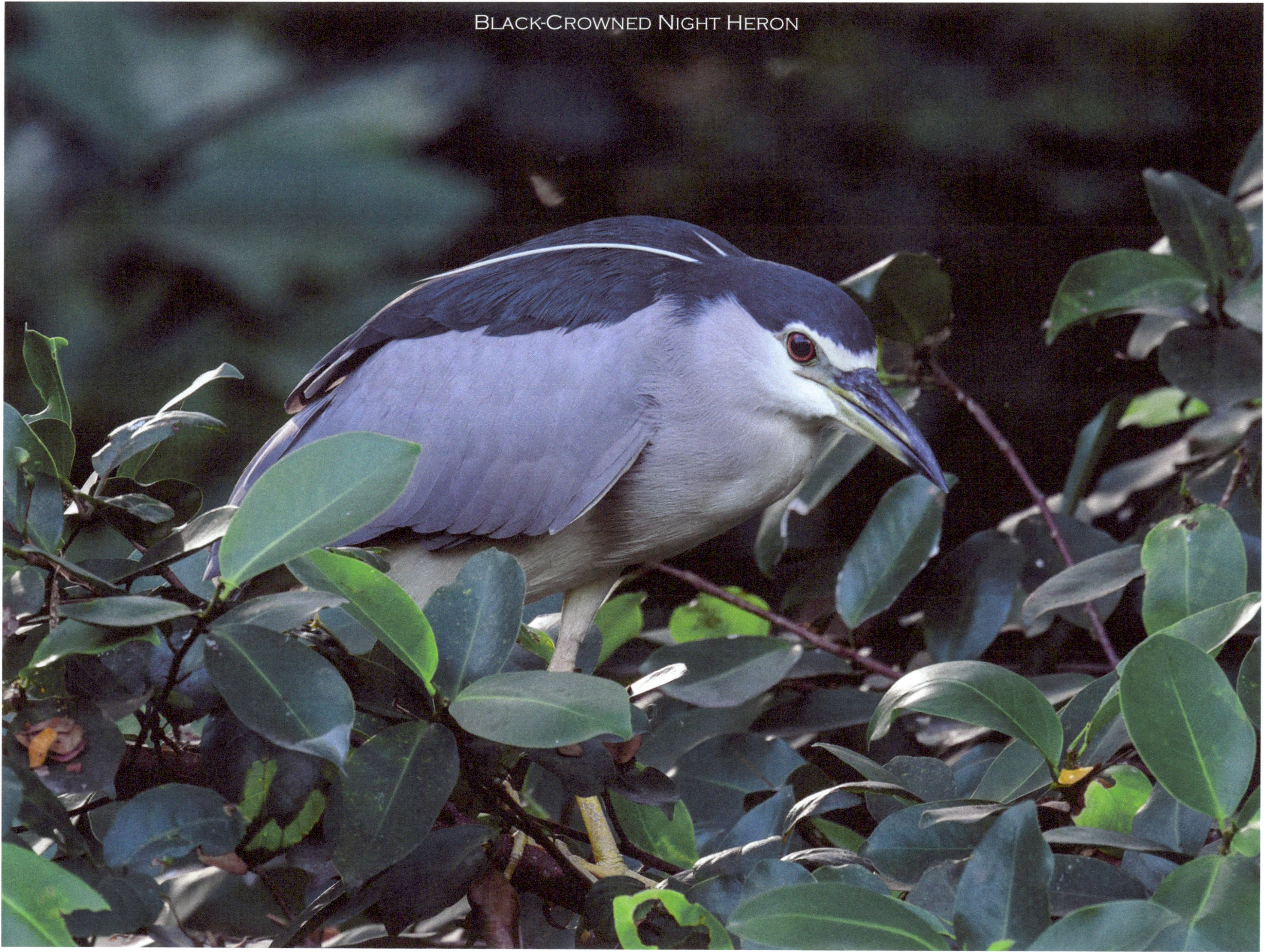

Black-Crowned Night Heron

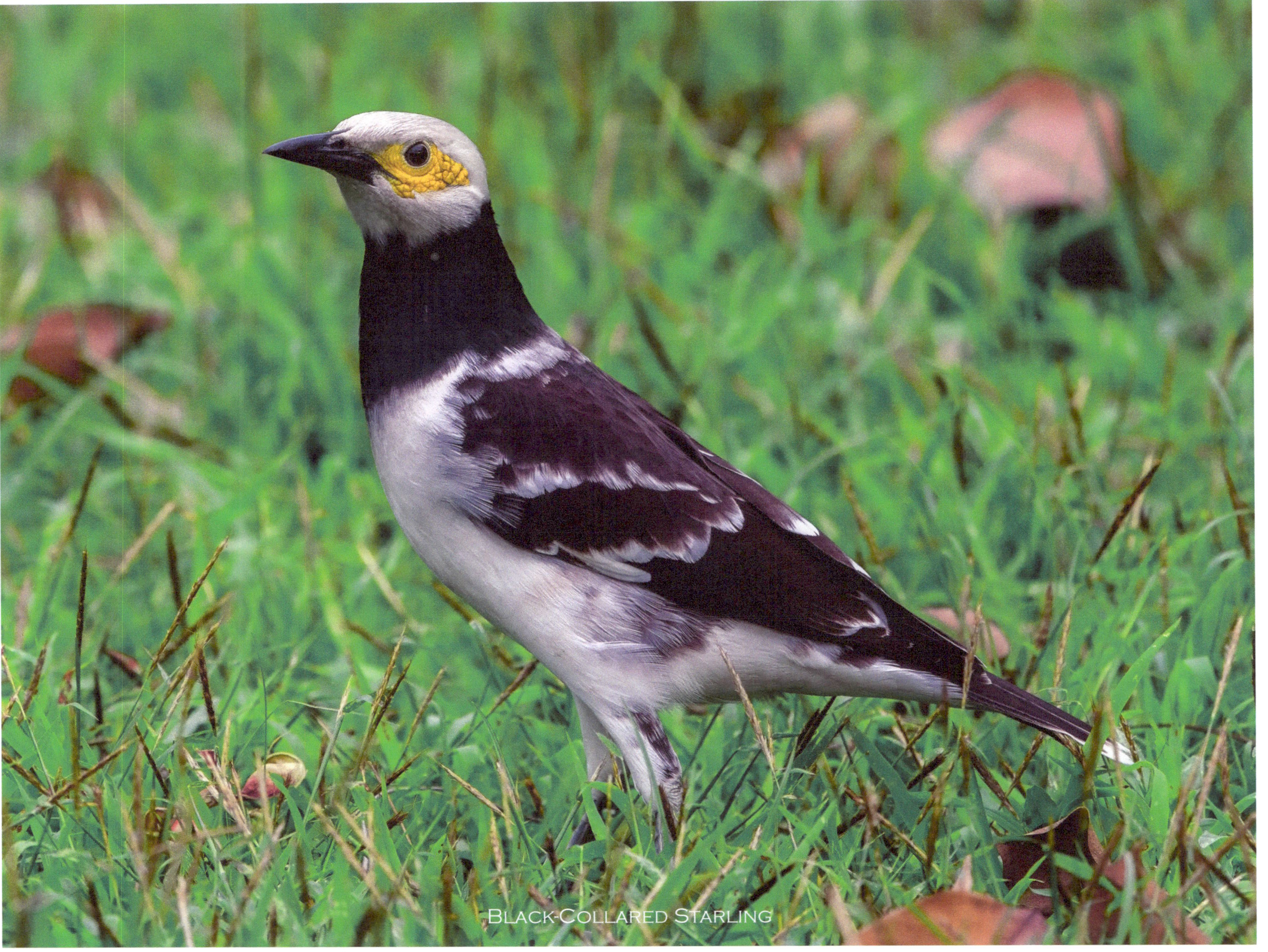
Black-Collared Starling

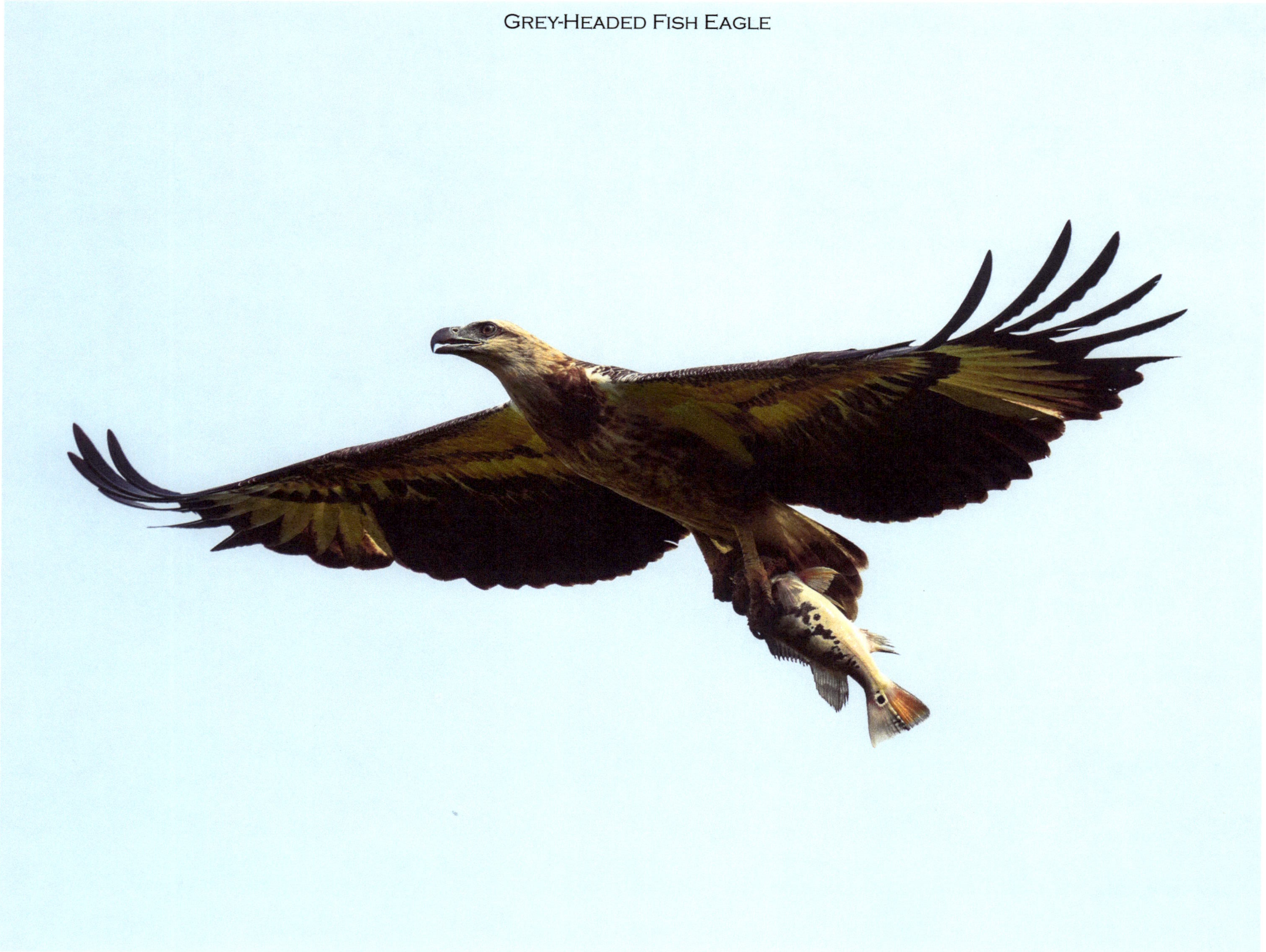

Grey-Headed Fish Eagle

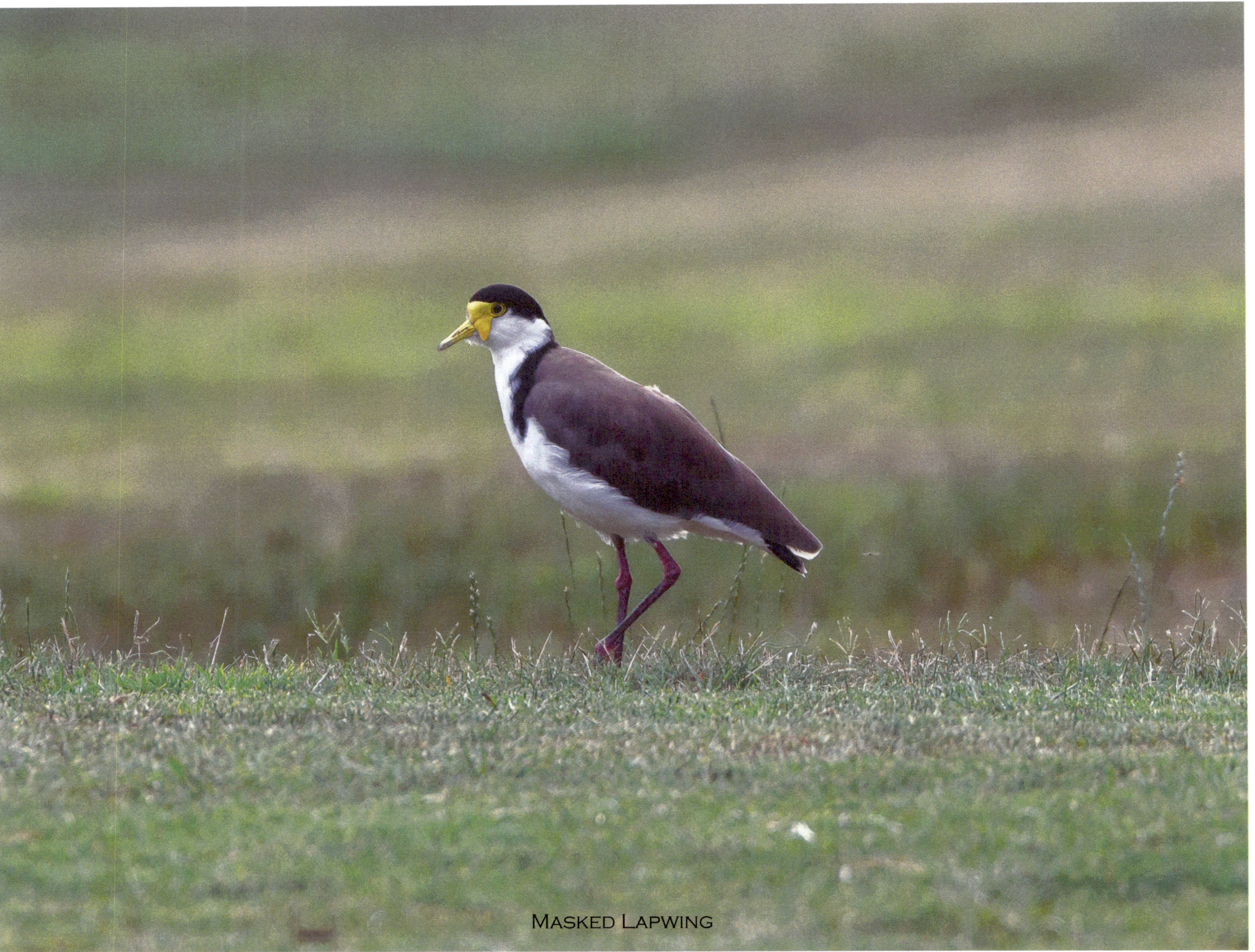

Masked Lapwing

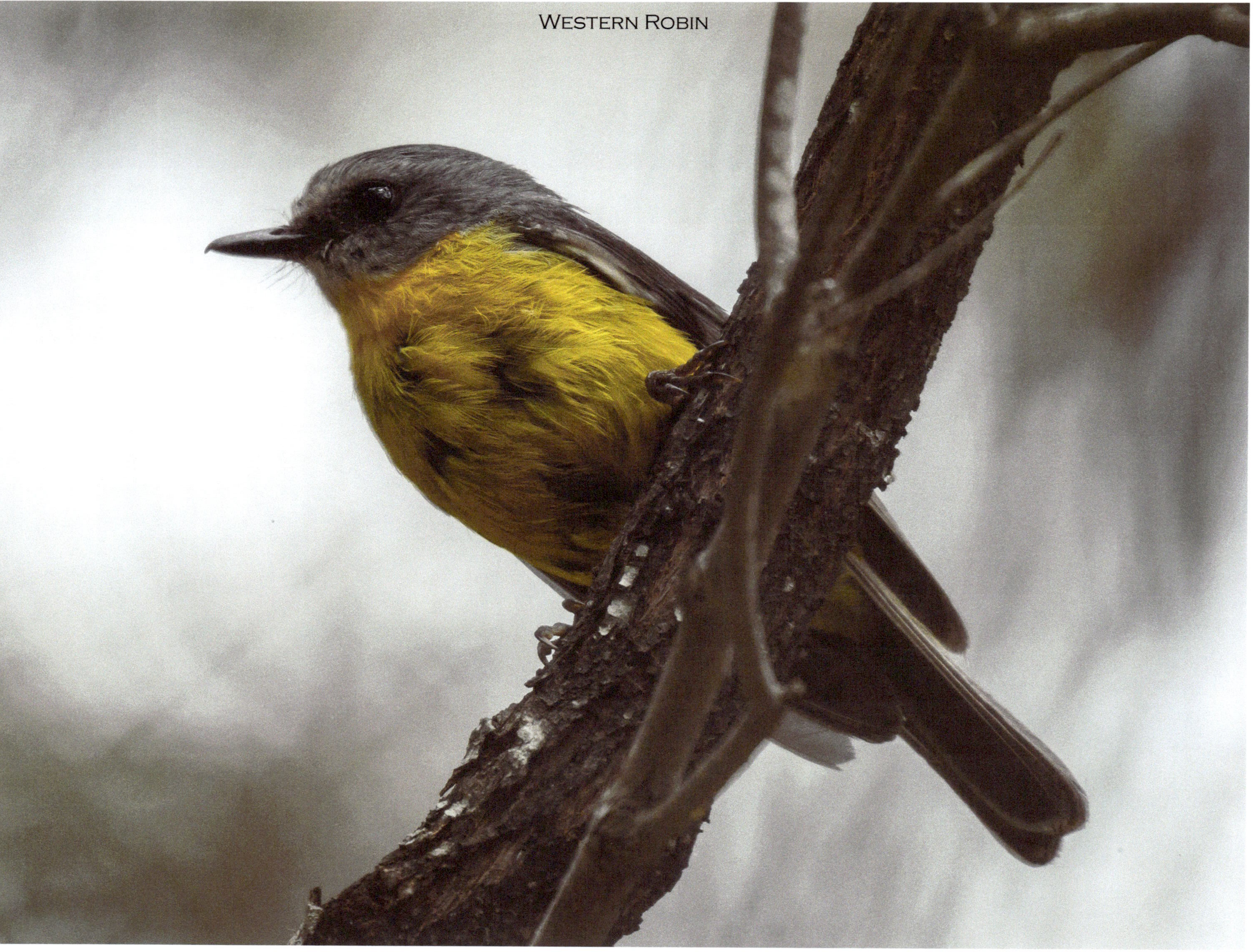

Western Robin

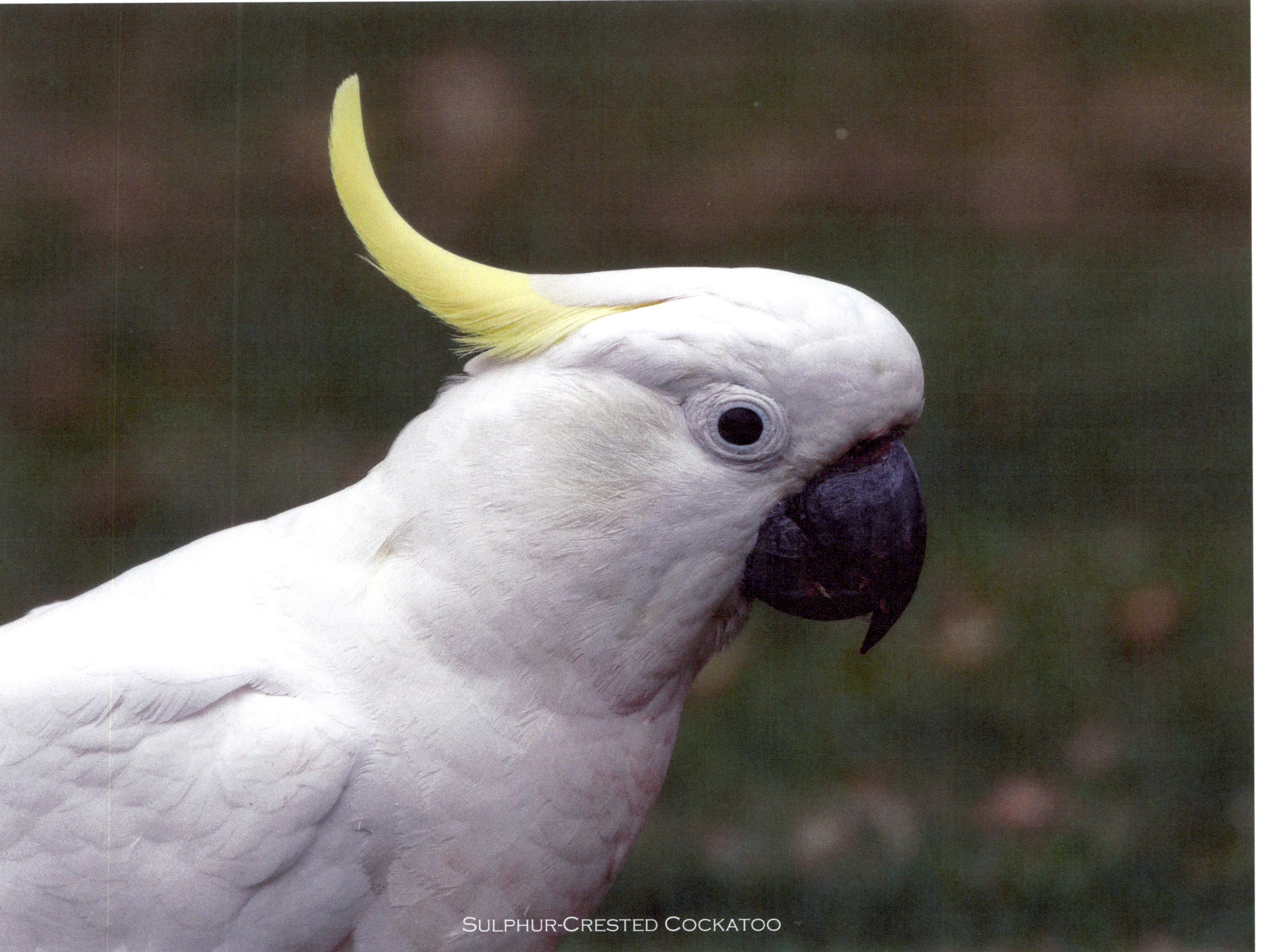

Sulphur-Crested Cockatoo

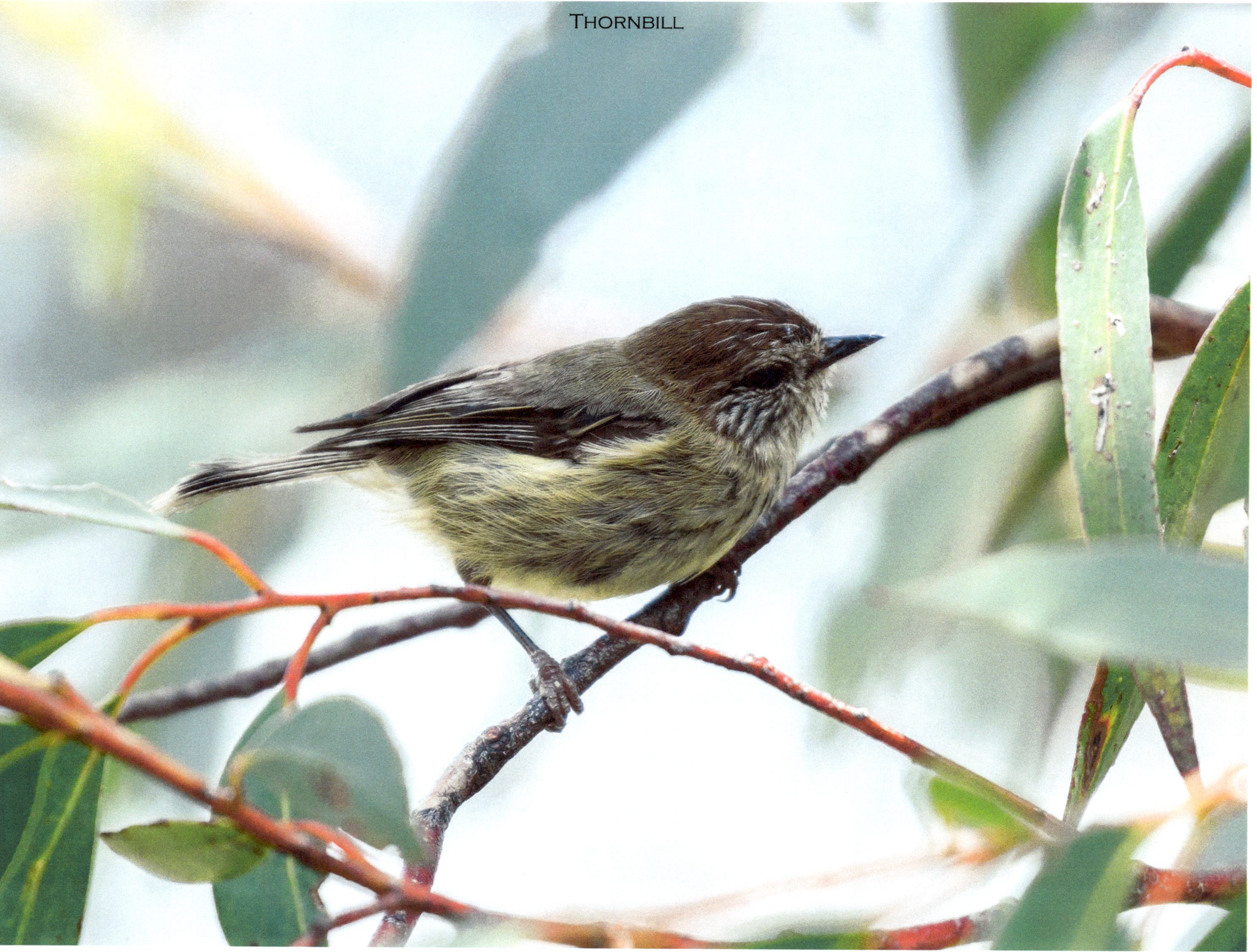

Thornbill

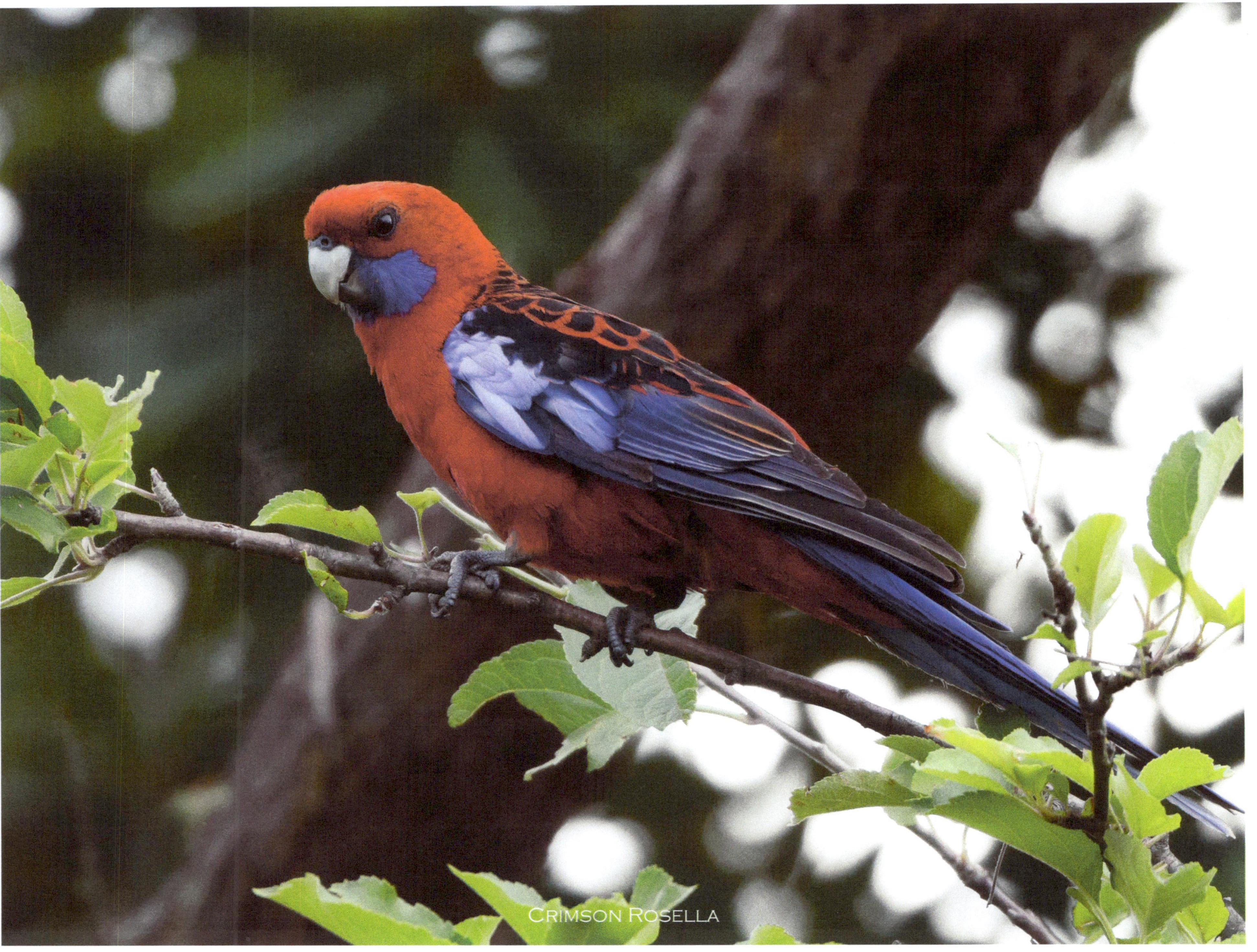

Crimson Rosella

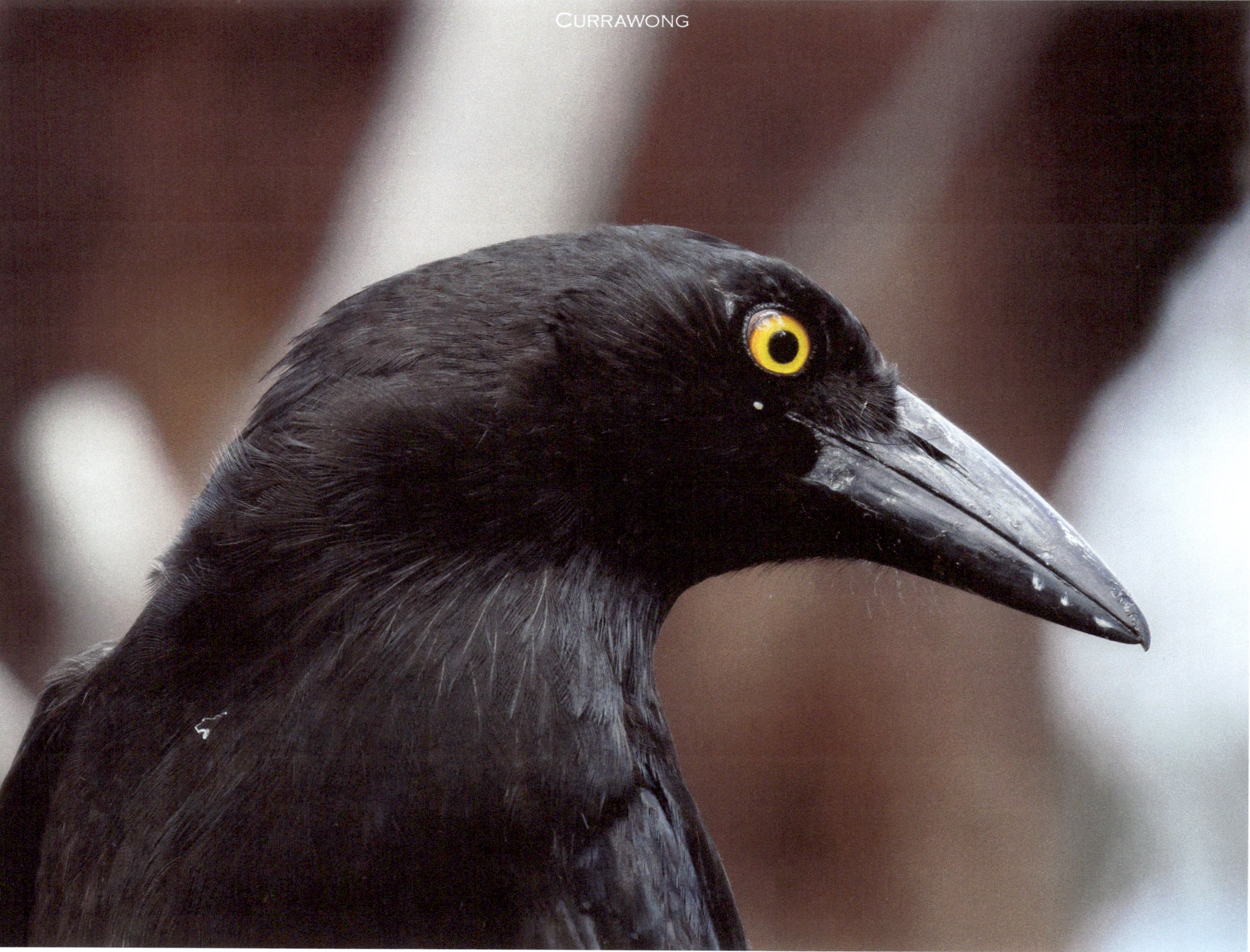

CURRAWONG

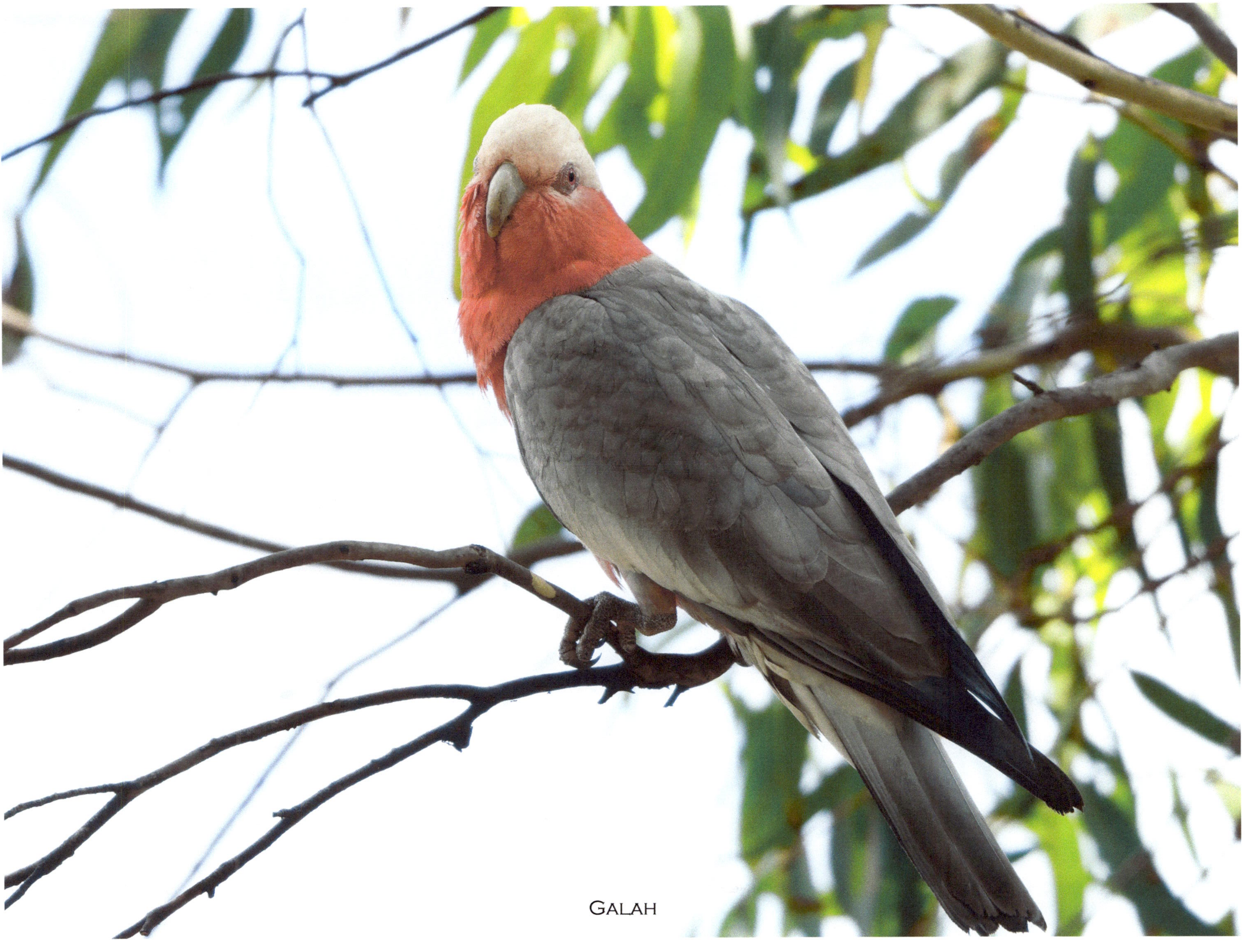

Galah

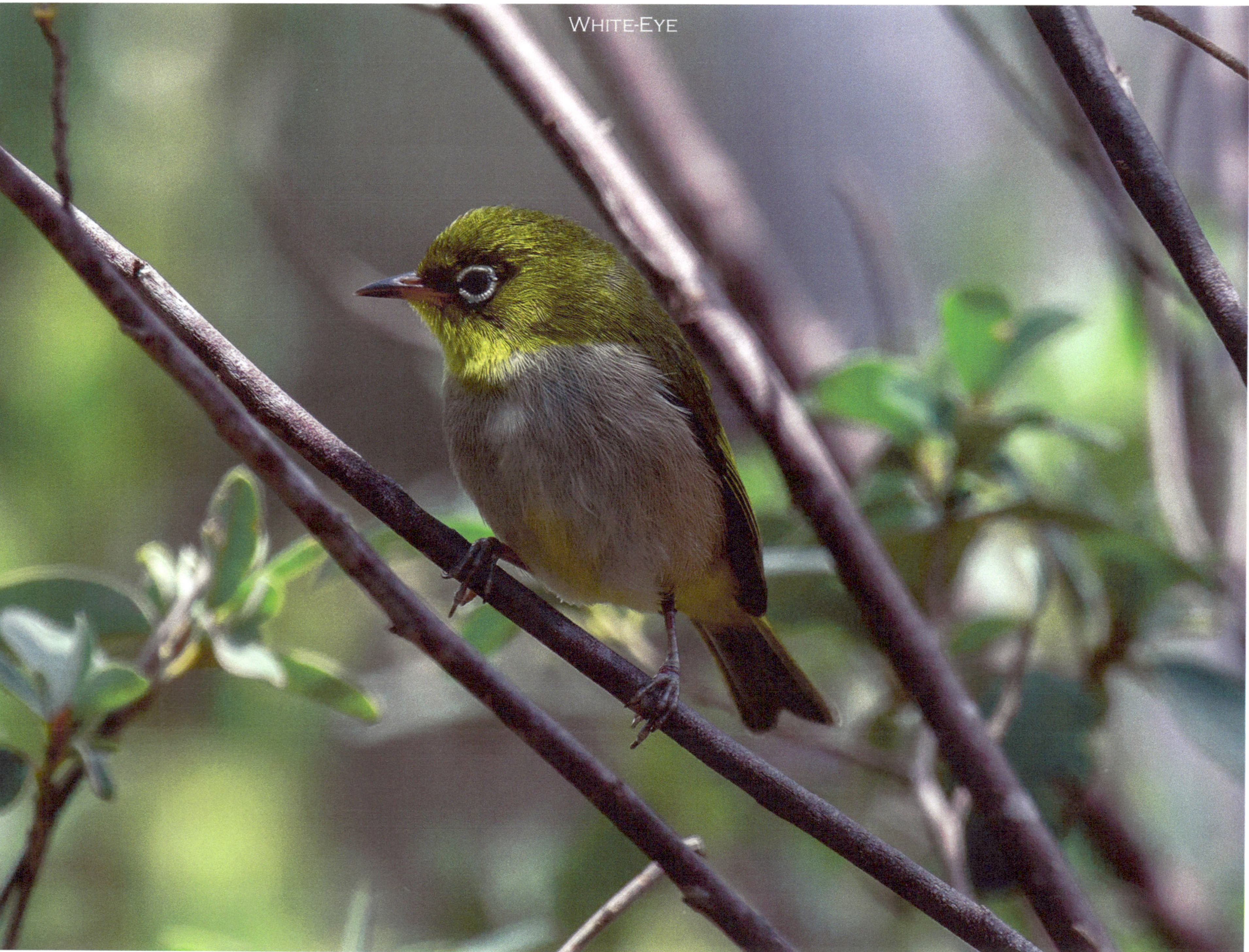

White-Eye

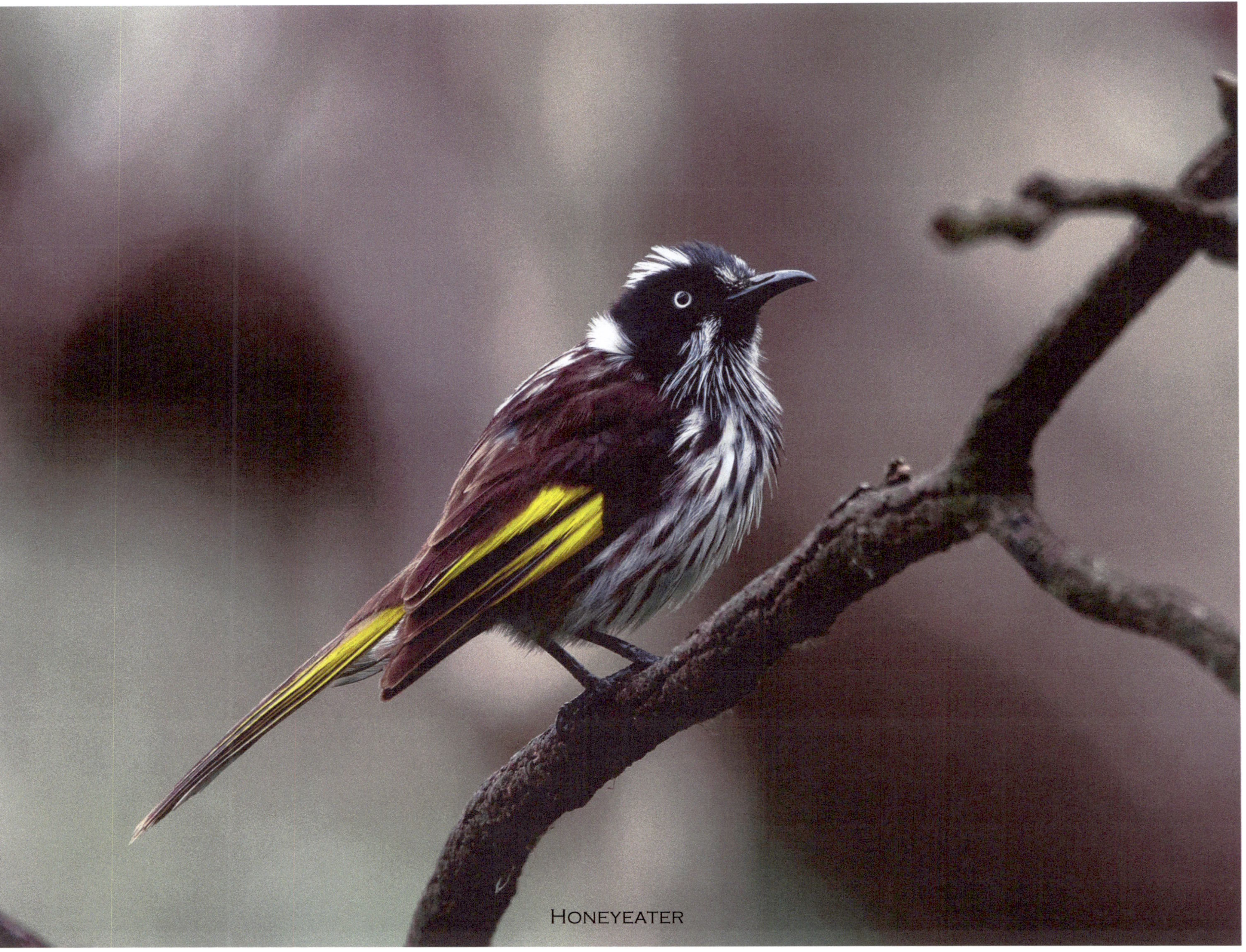

HONEYEATER

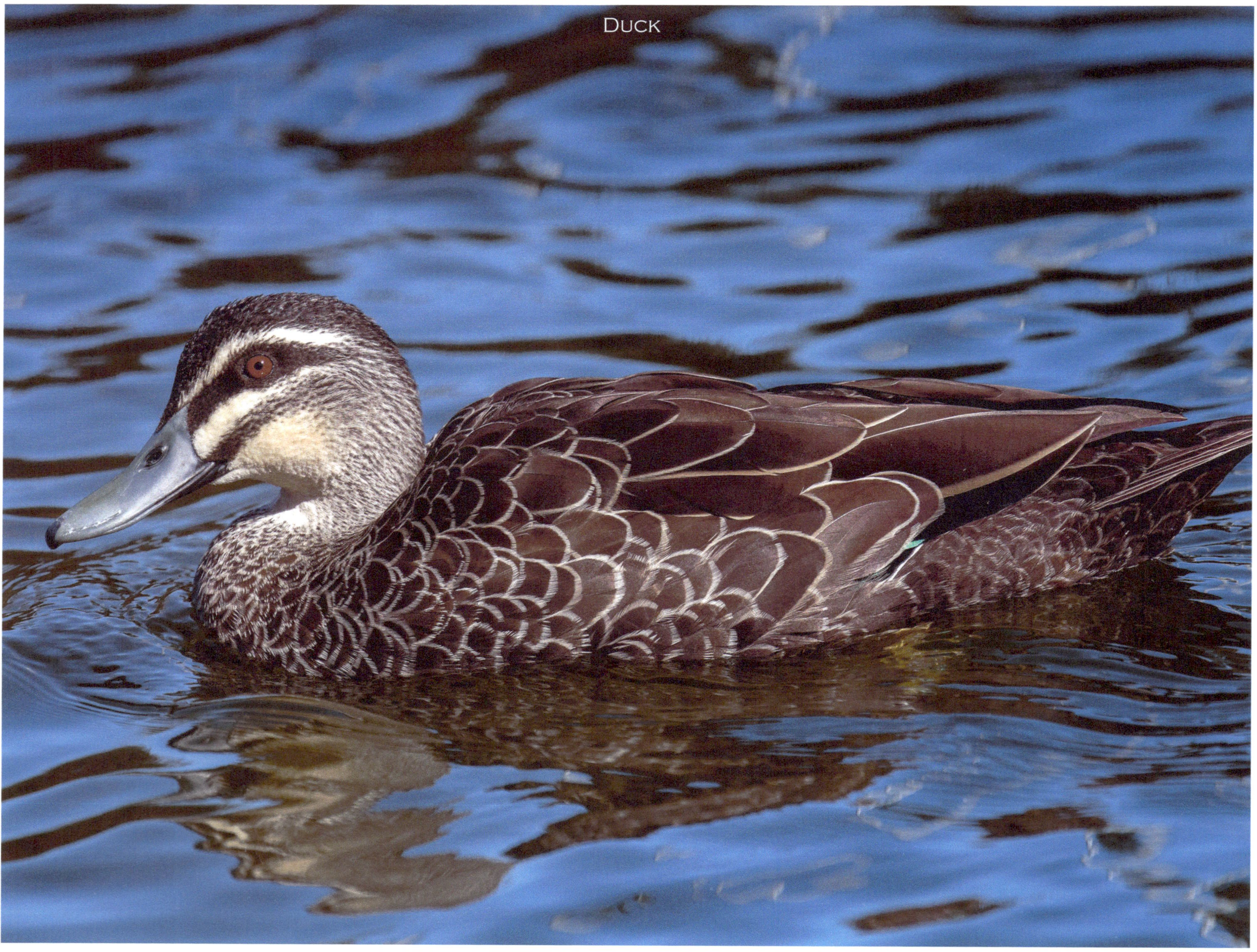

Duck

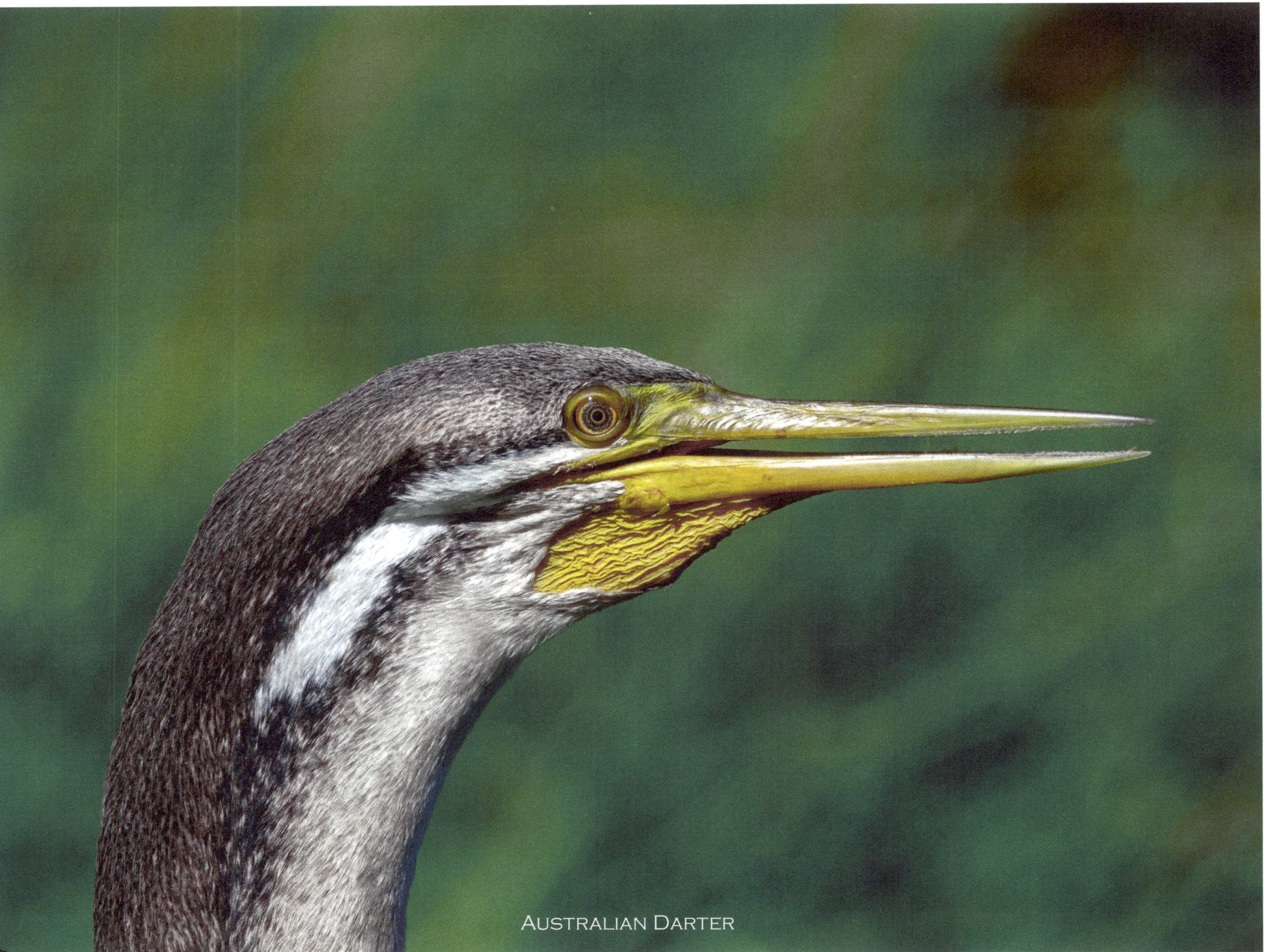

Australian Darter

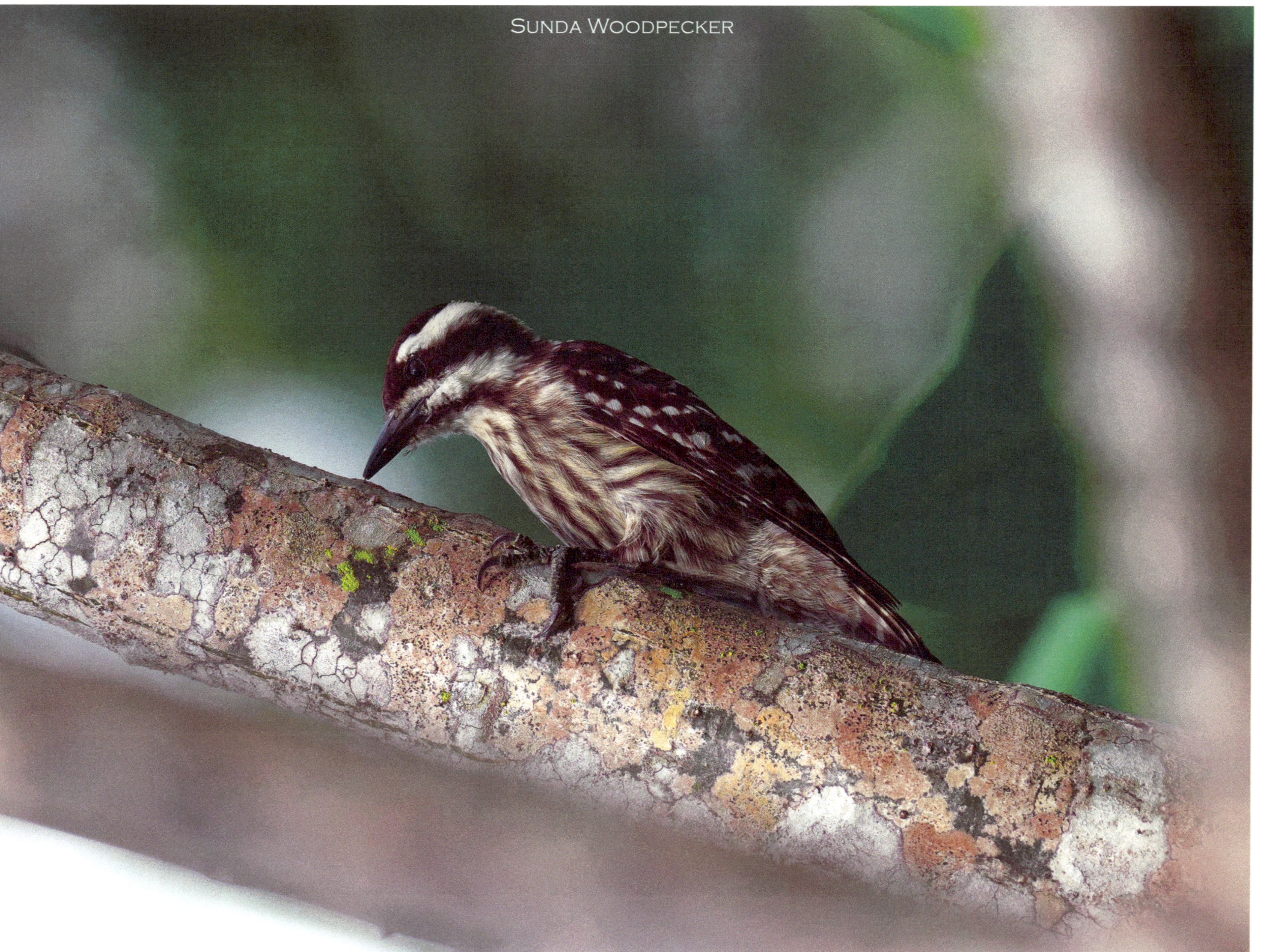

Sunda Woodpecker

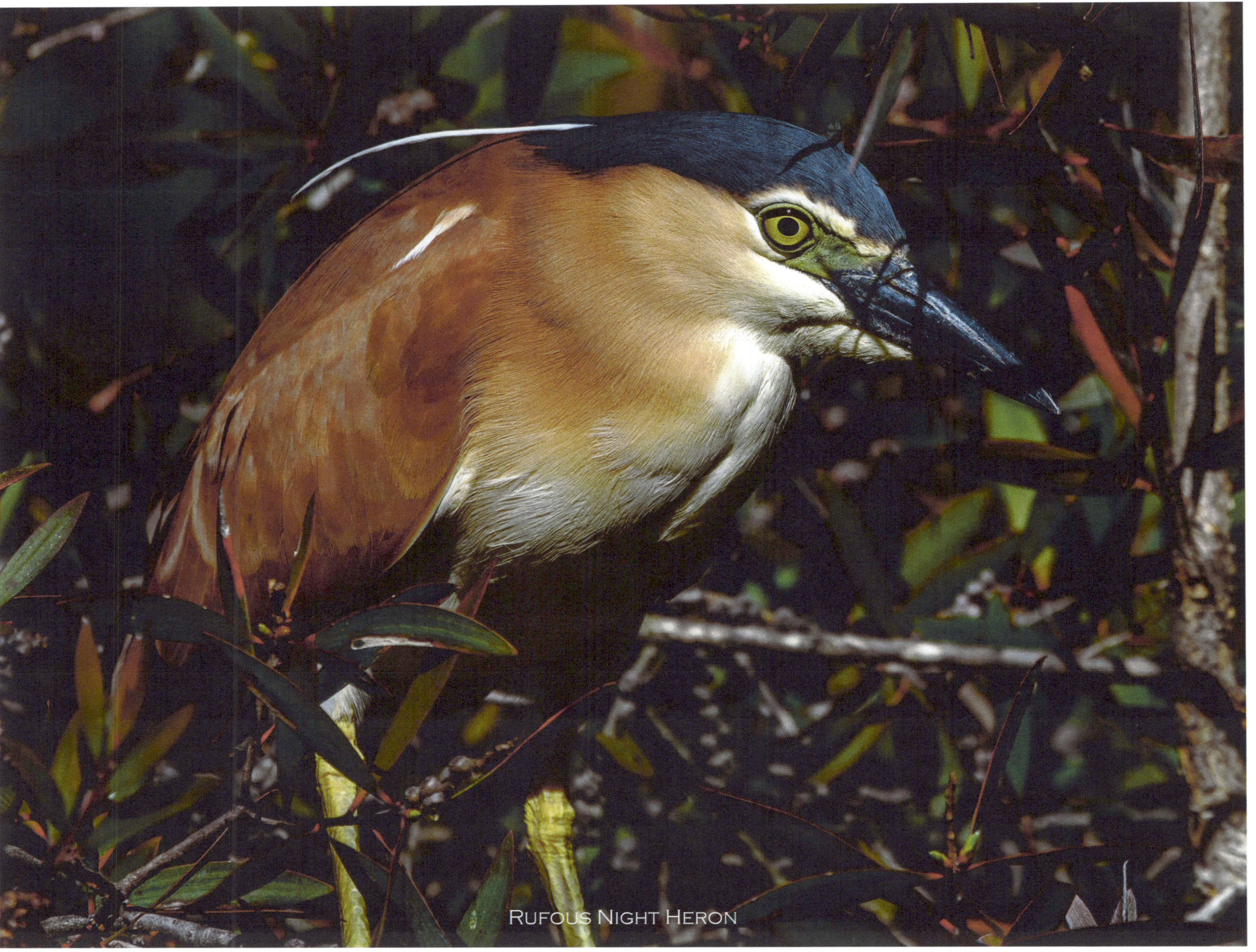

Rufous Night Heron

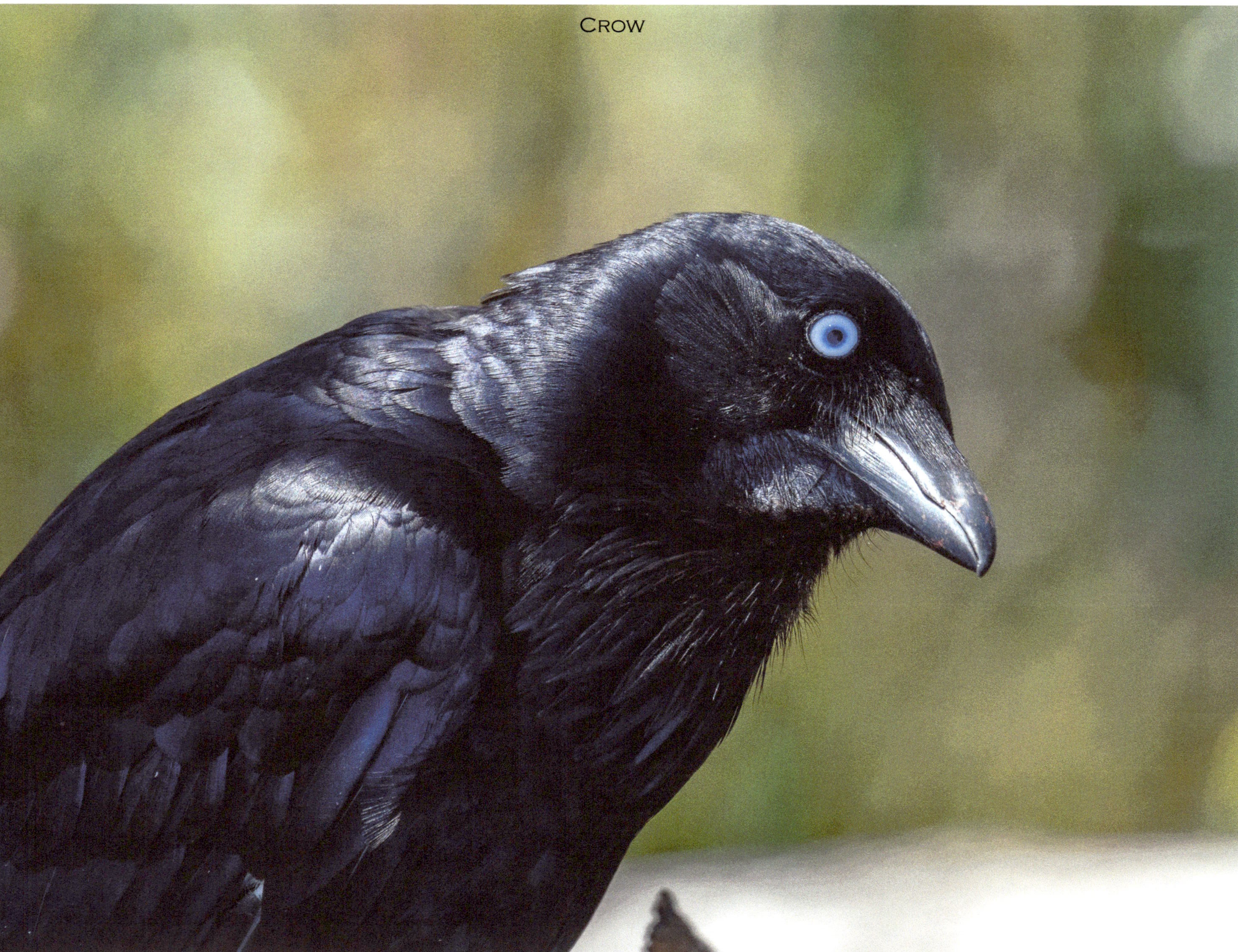

CROW

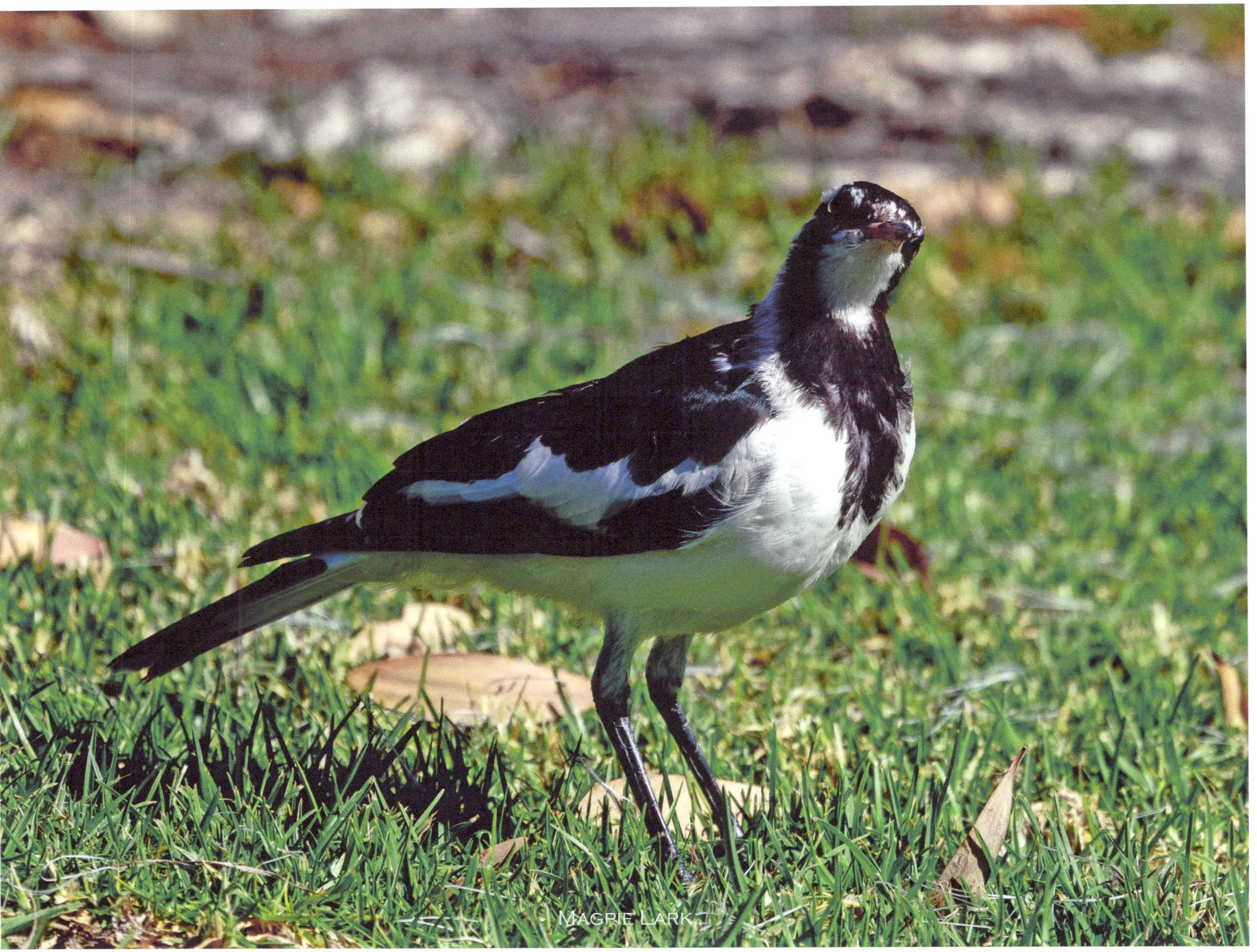
Magpie Lark

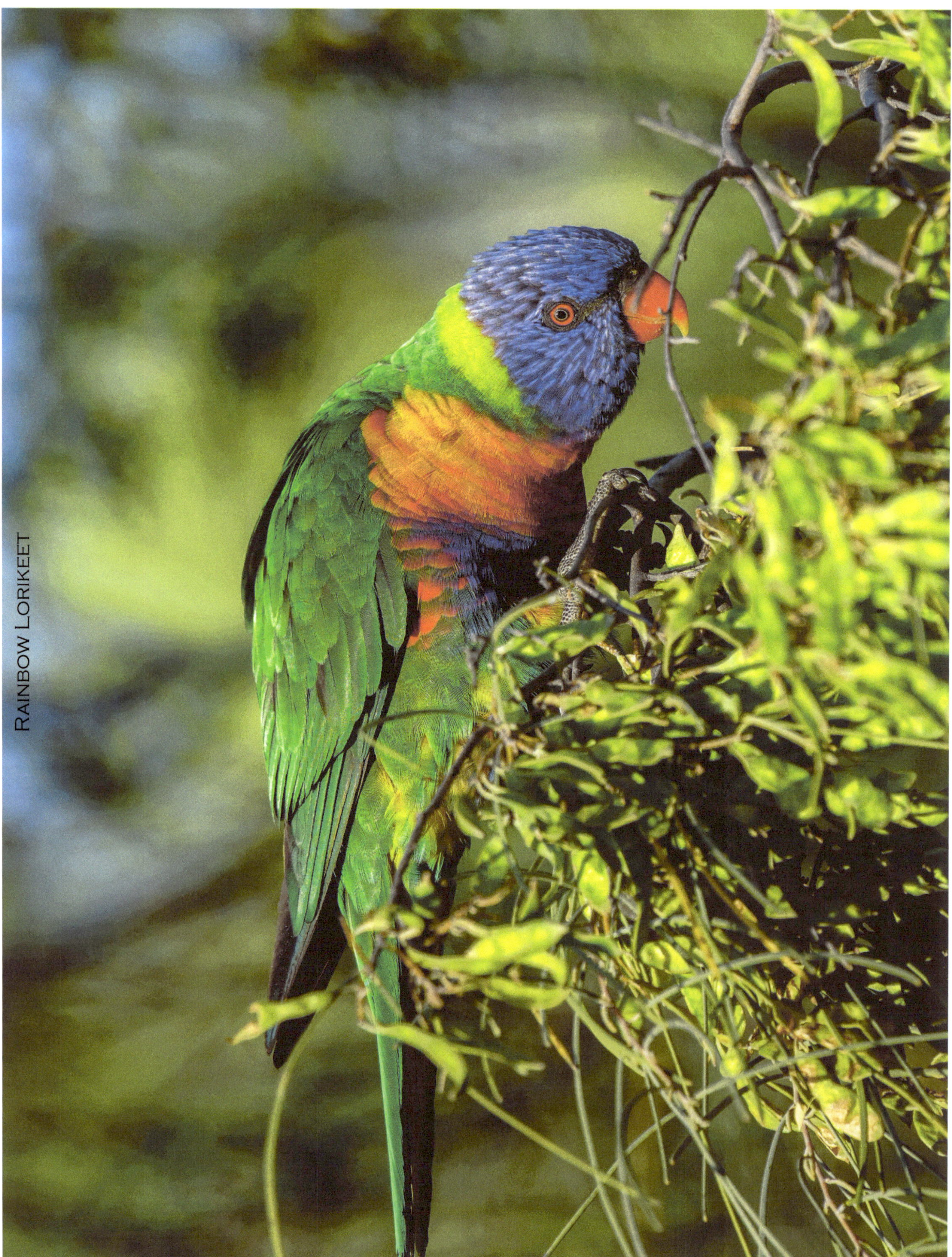

Rainbow Lorikeet

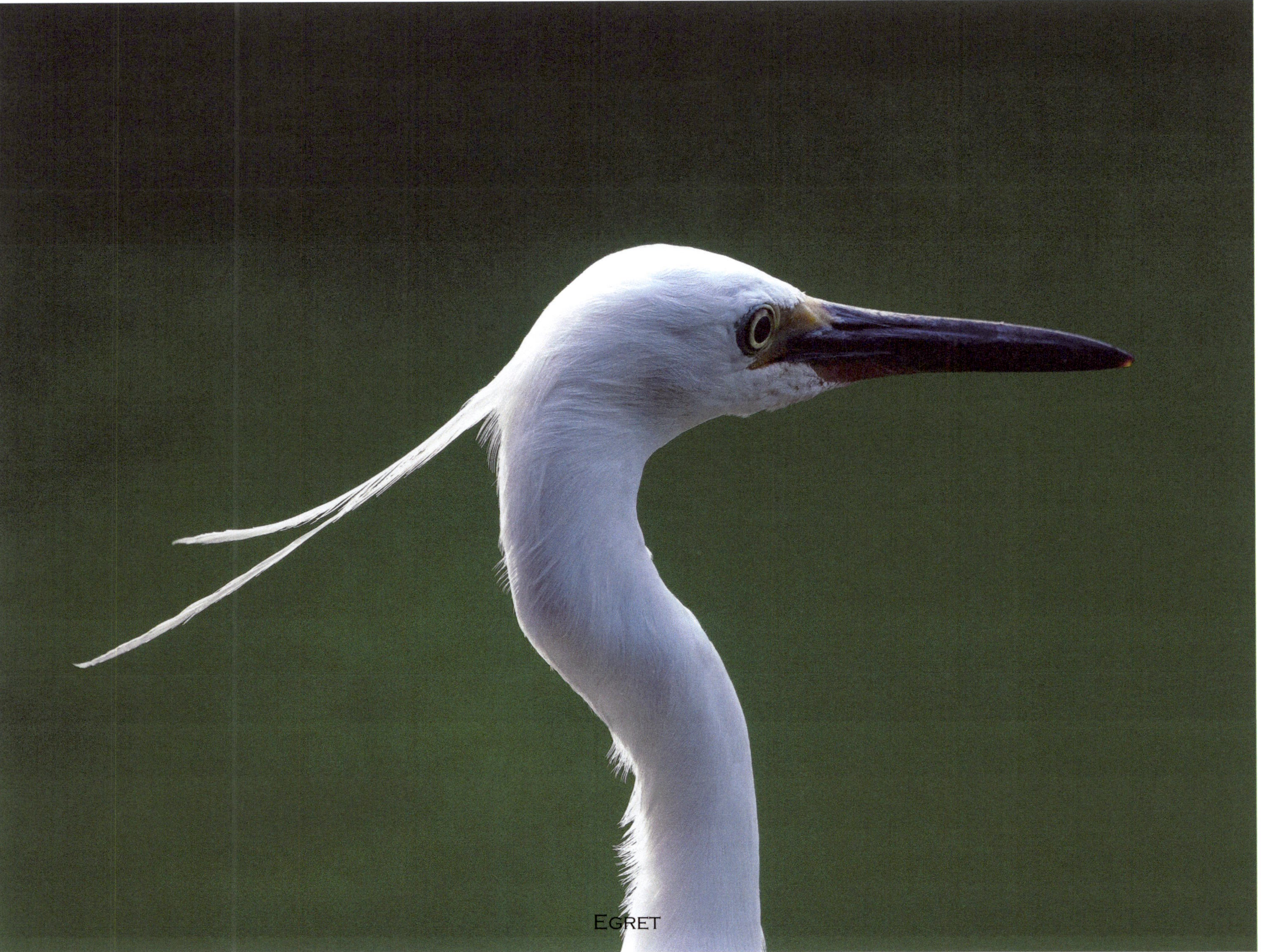

Egret

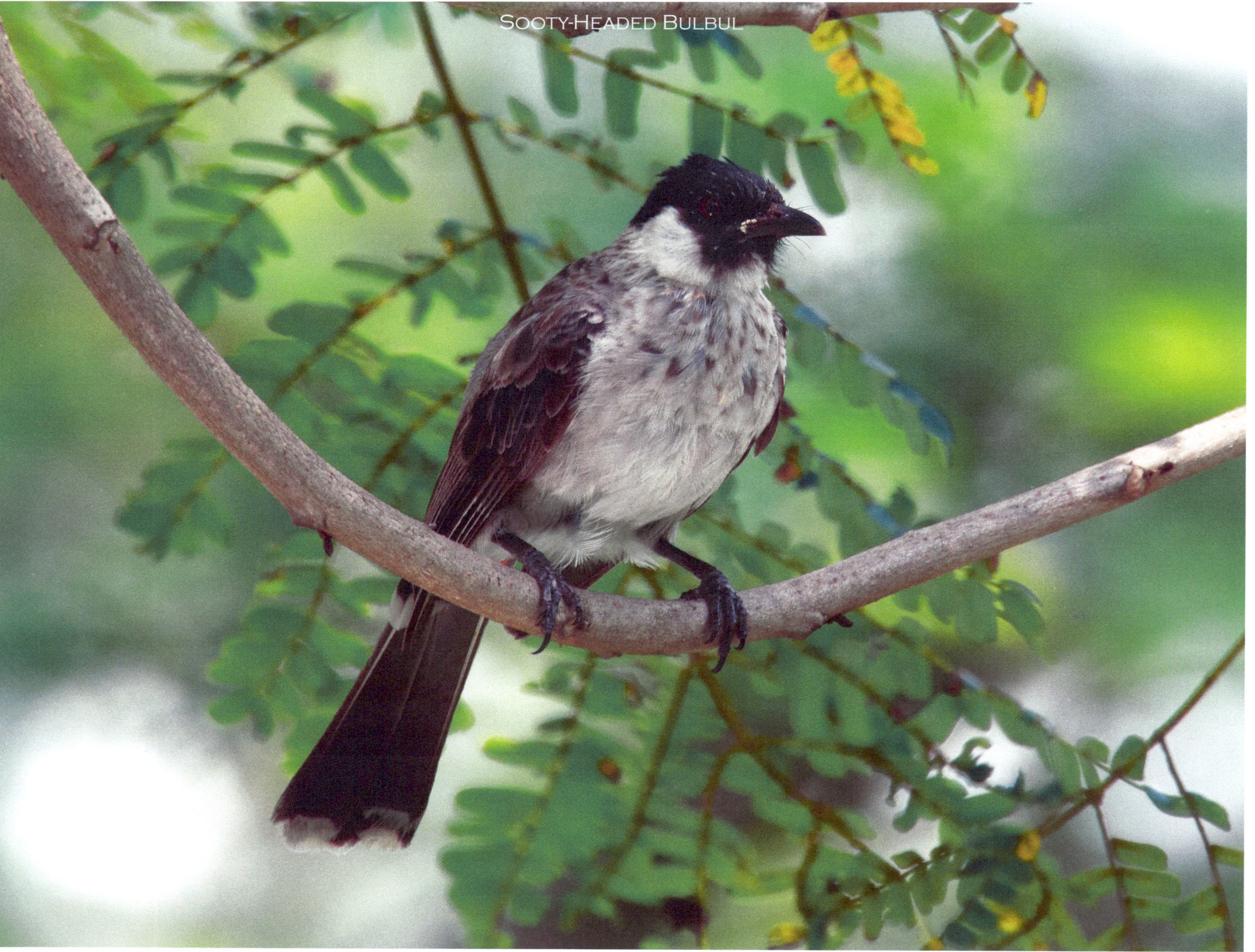

Sooty-Headed Bulbul

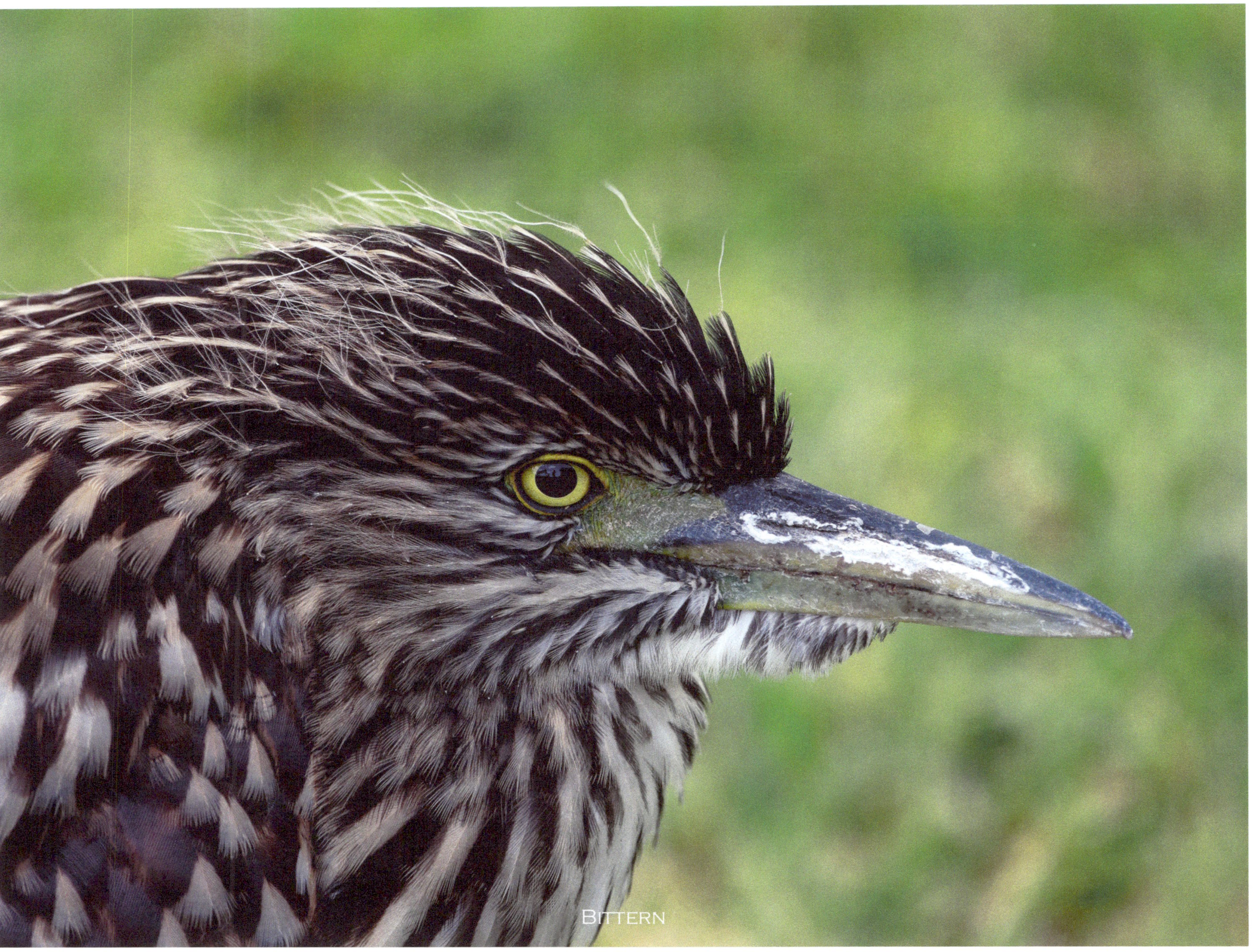

Bittern

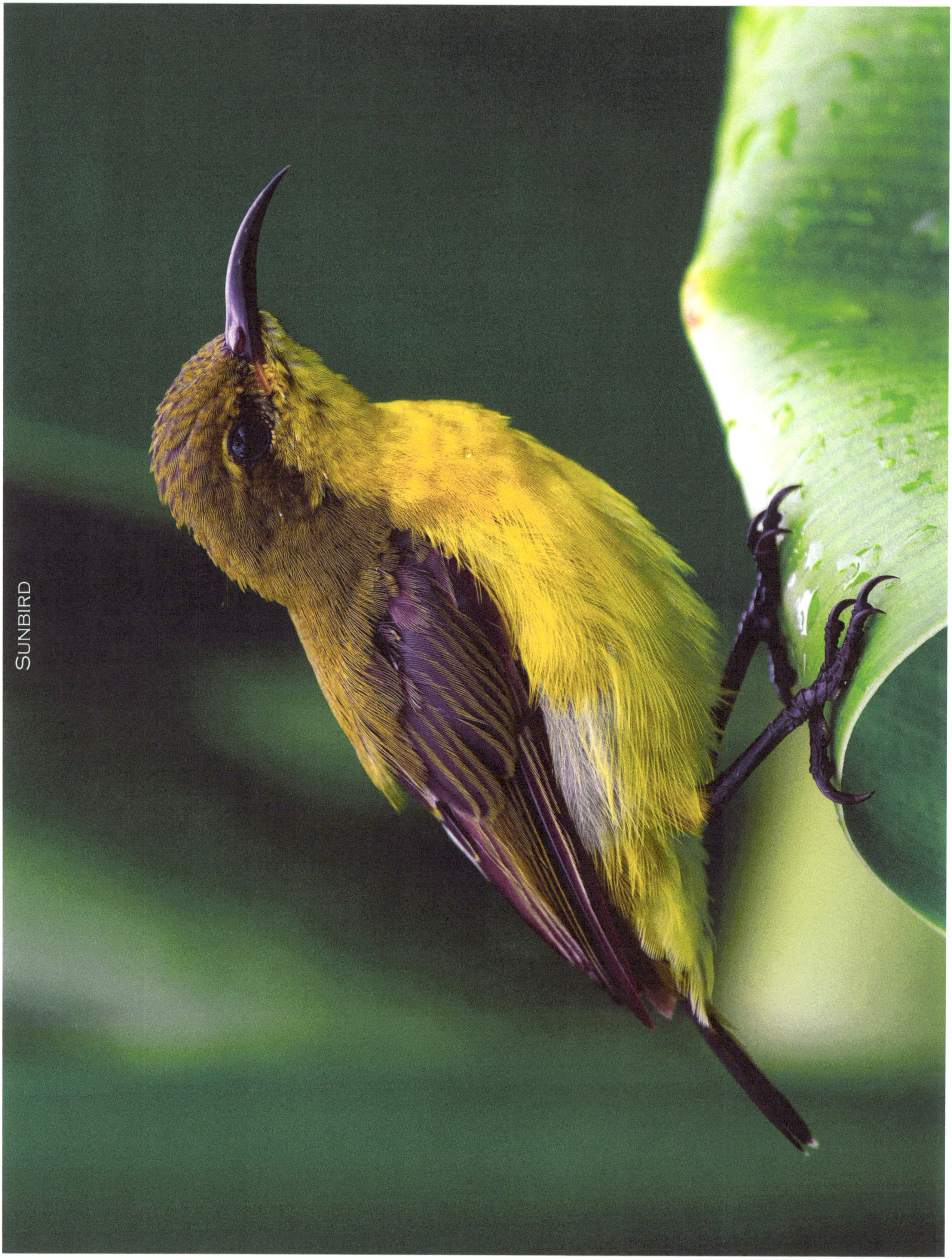

Sunbird

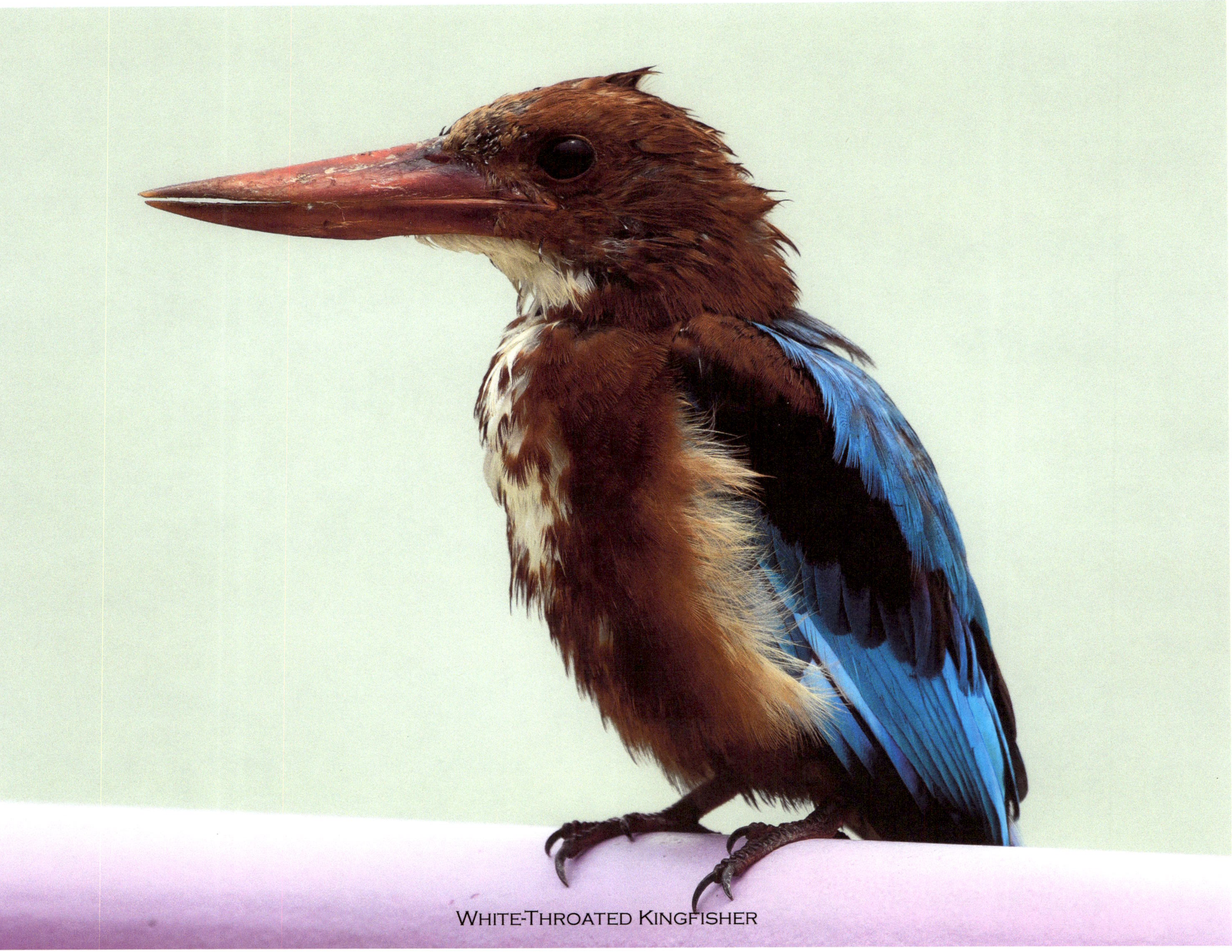

White-Throated Kingfisher

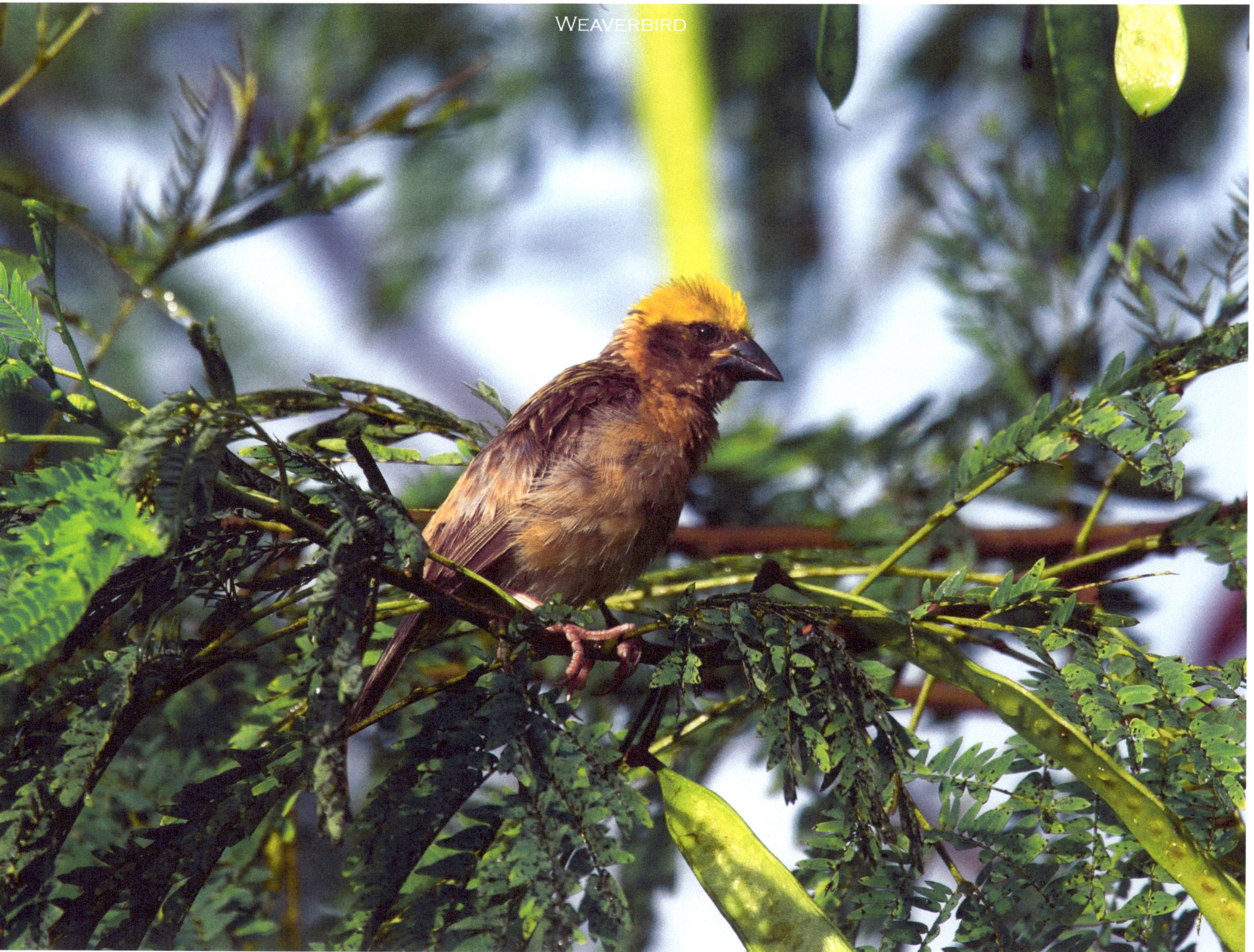

WEAVERBIRD

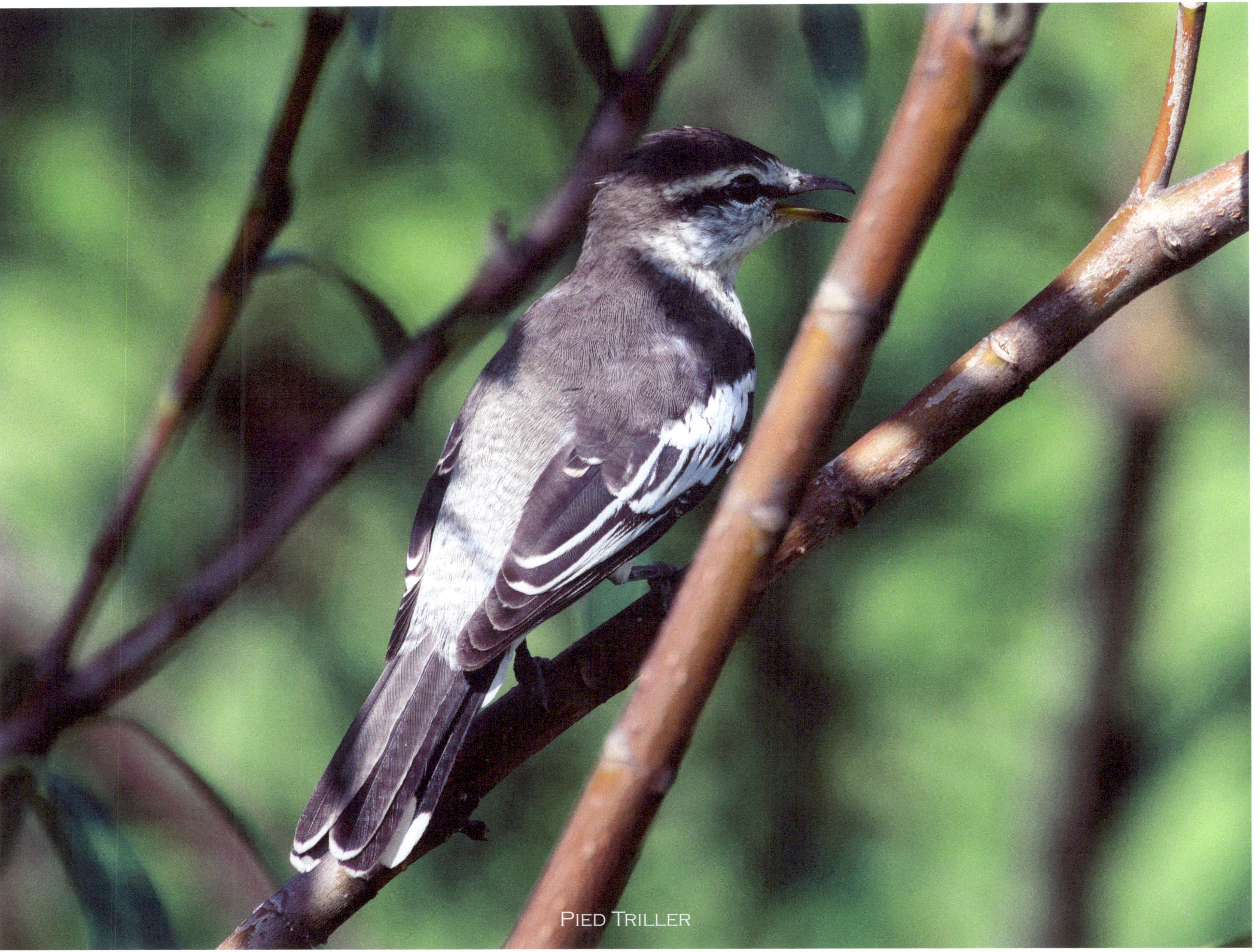

Pied Triller

Sunbird

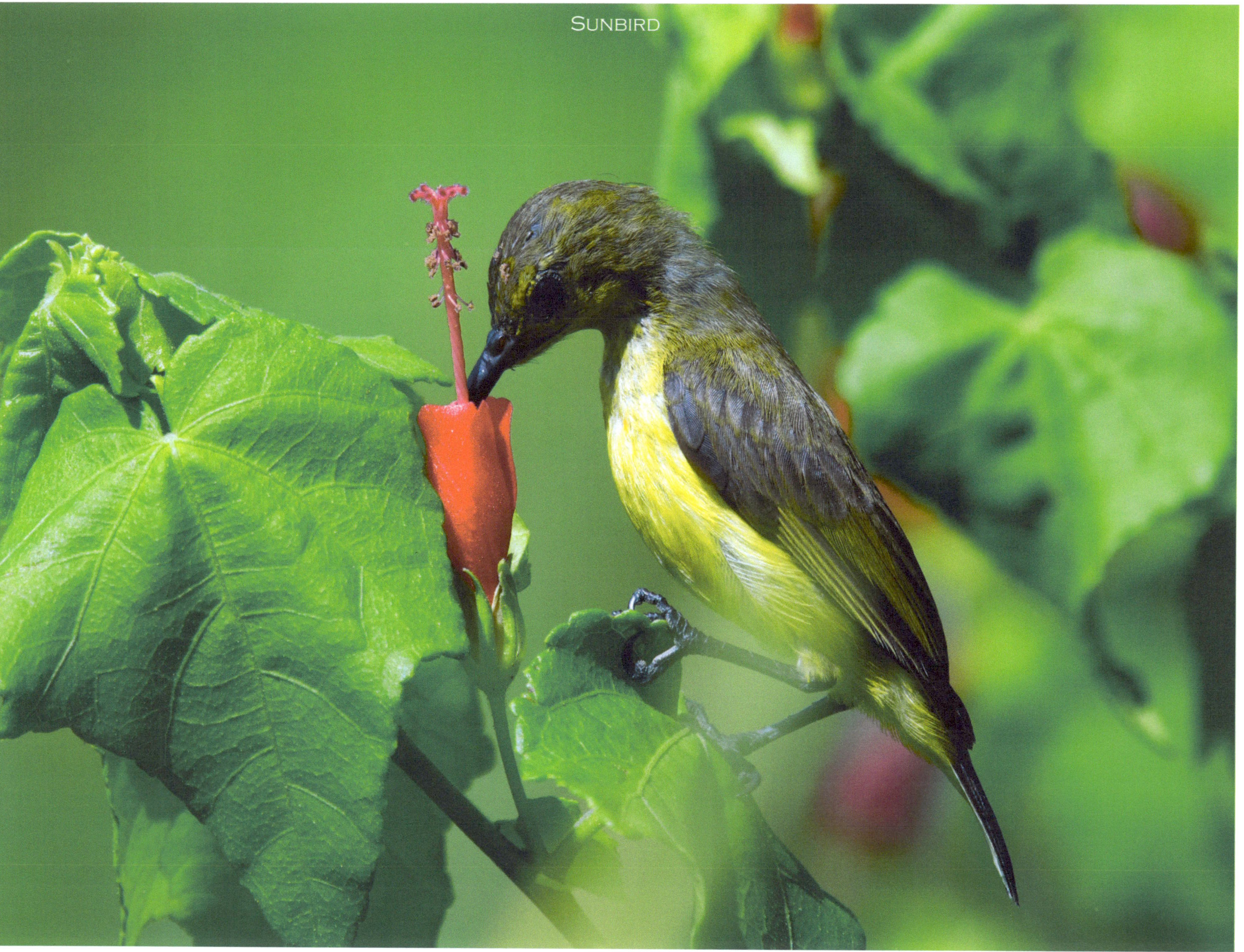

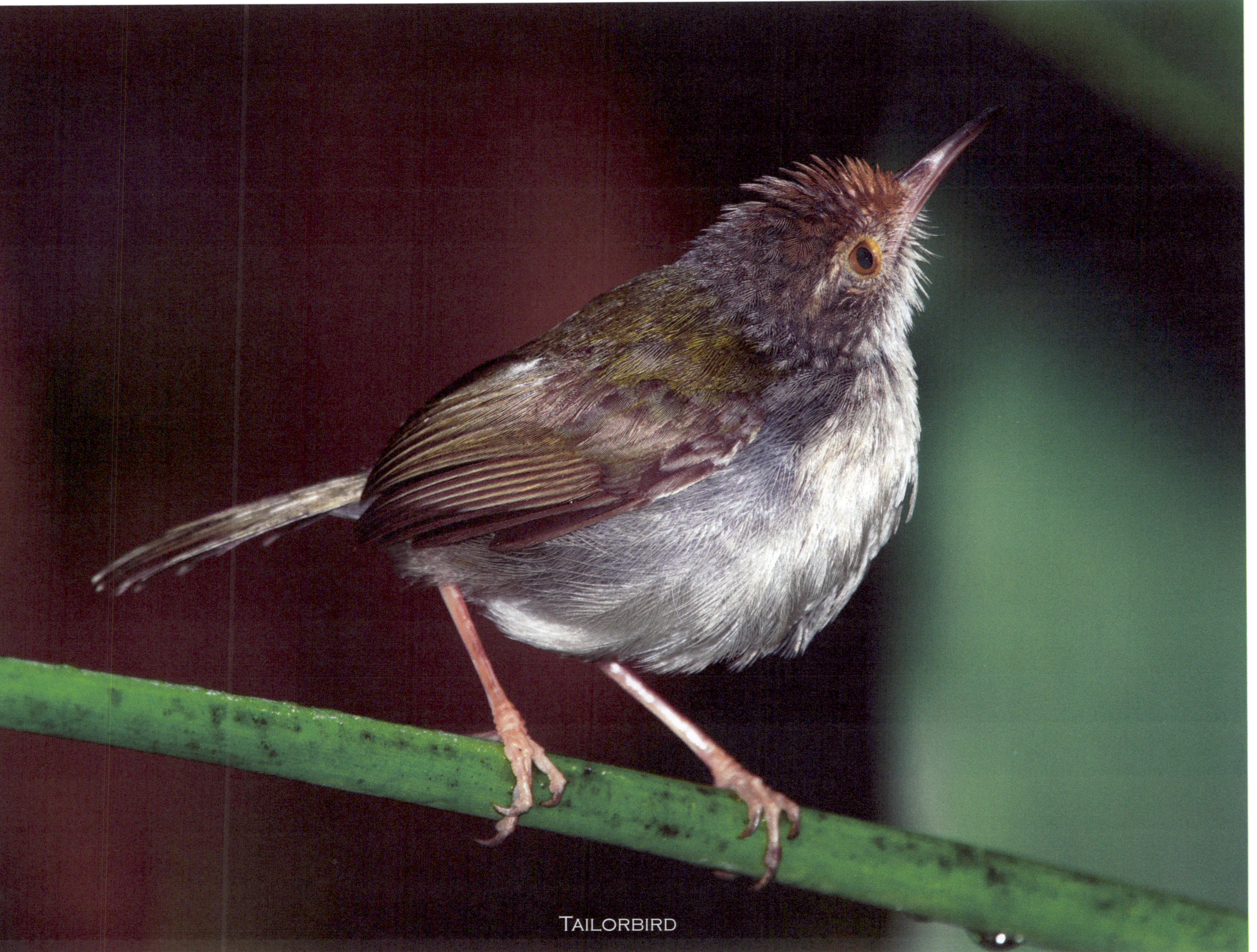

Tailorbird

Cormorant

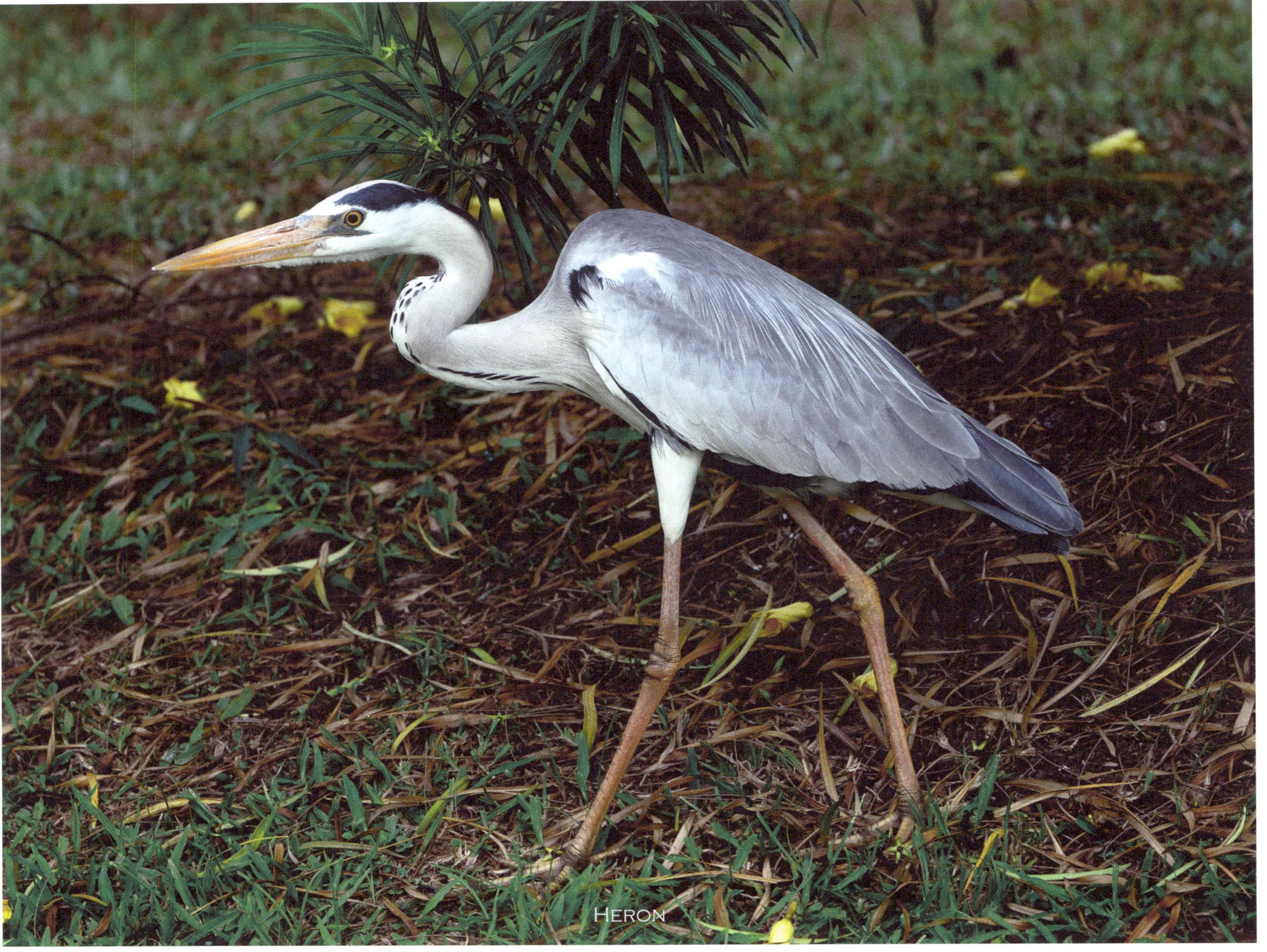

Heron

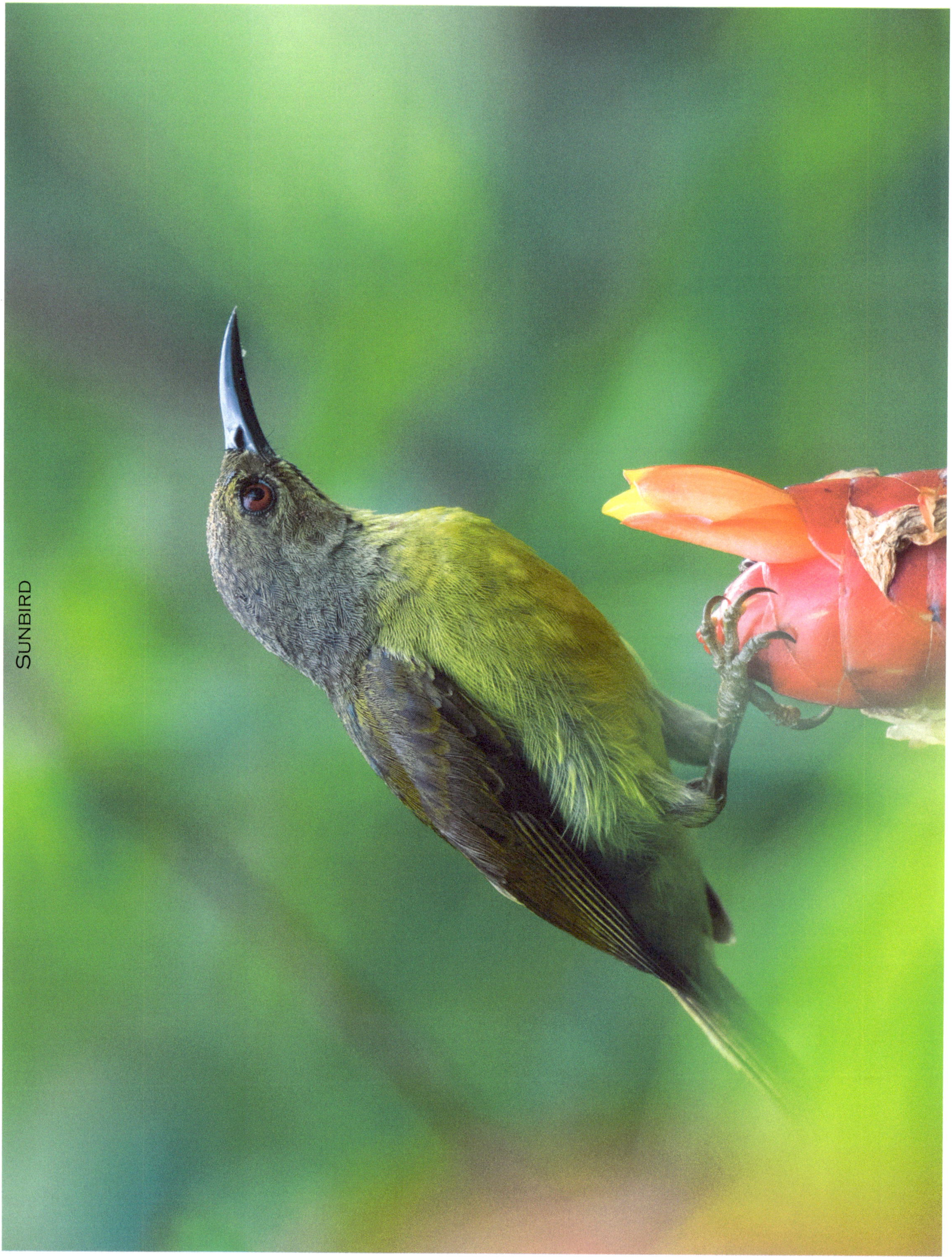

Sunbird

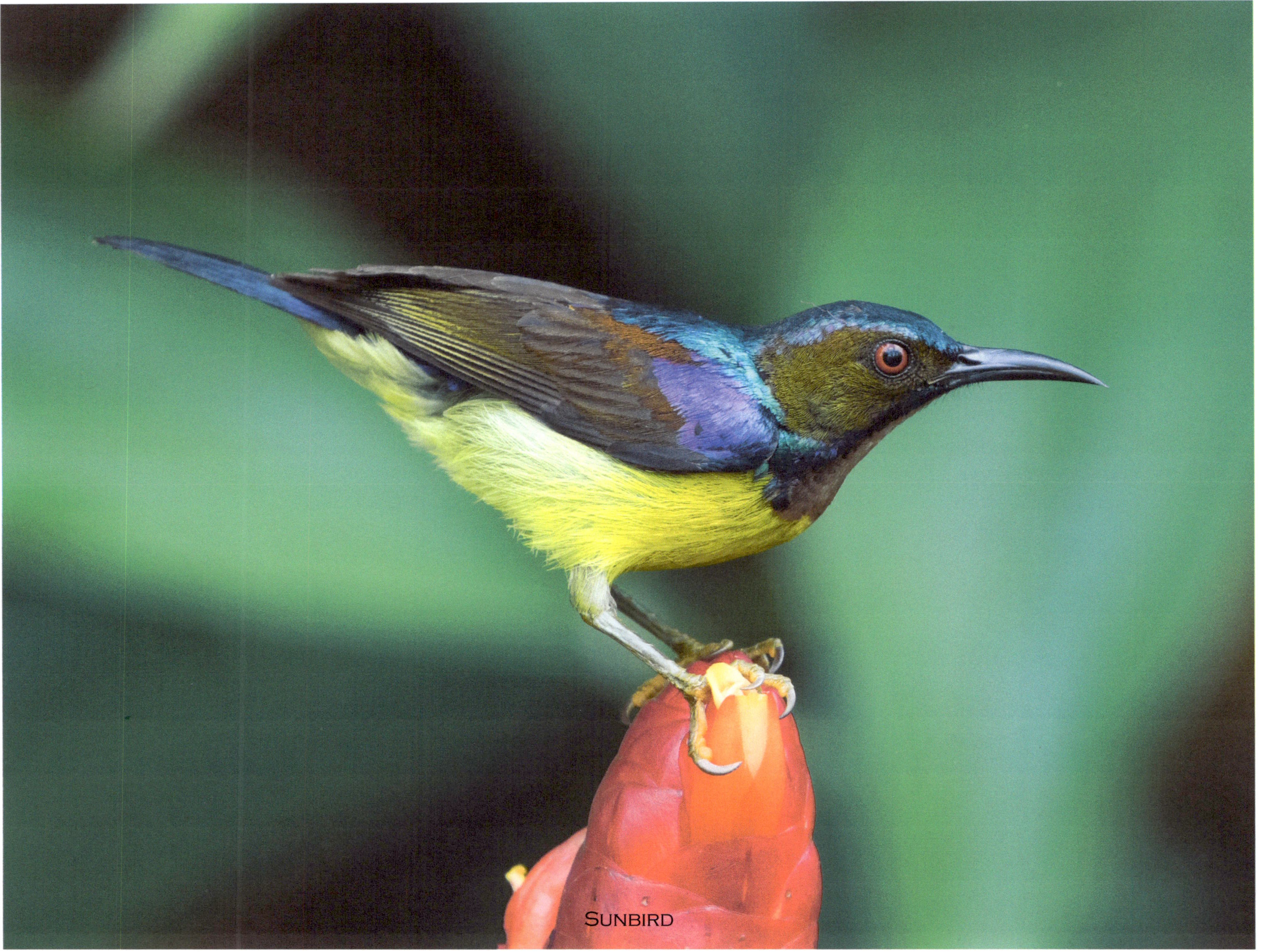
SUNBIRD

Pacific Swallow

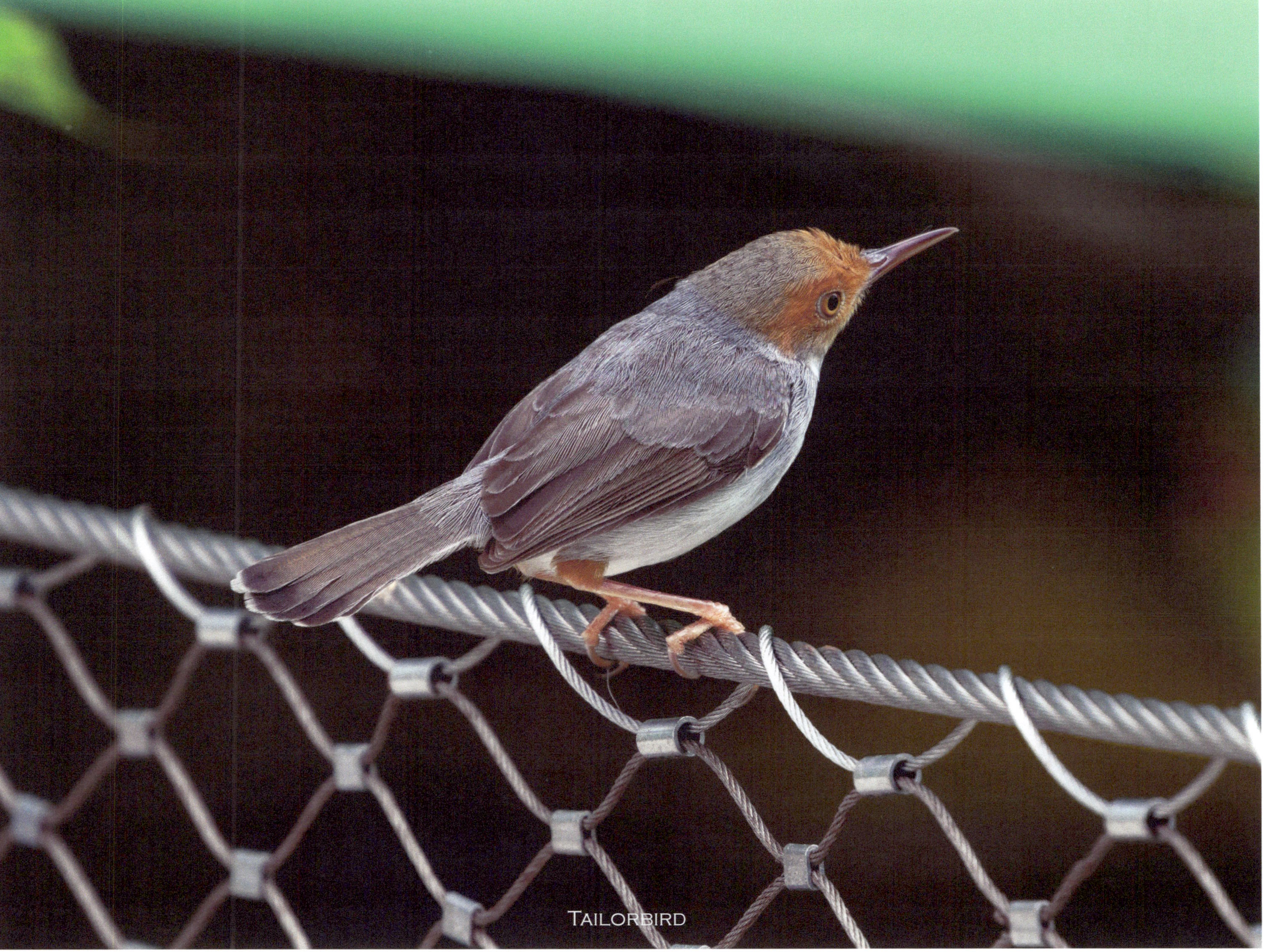

TAILORBIRD

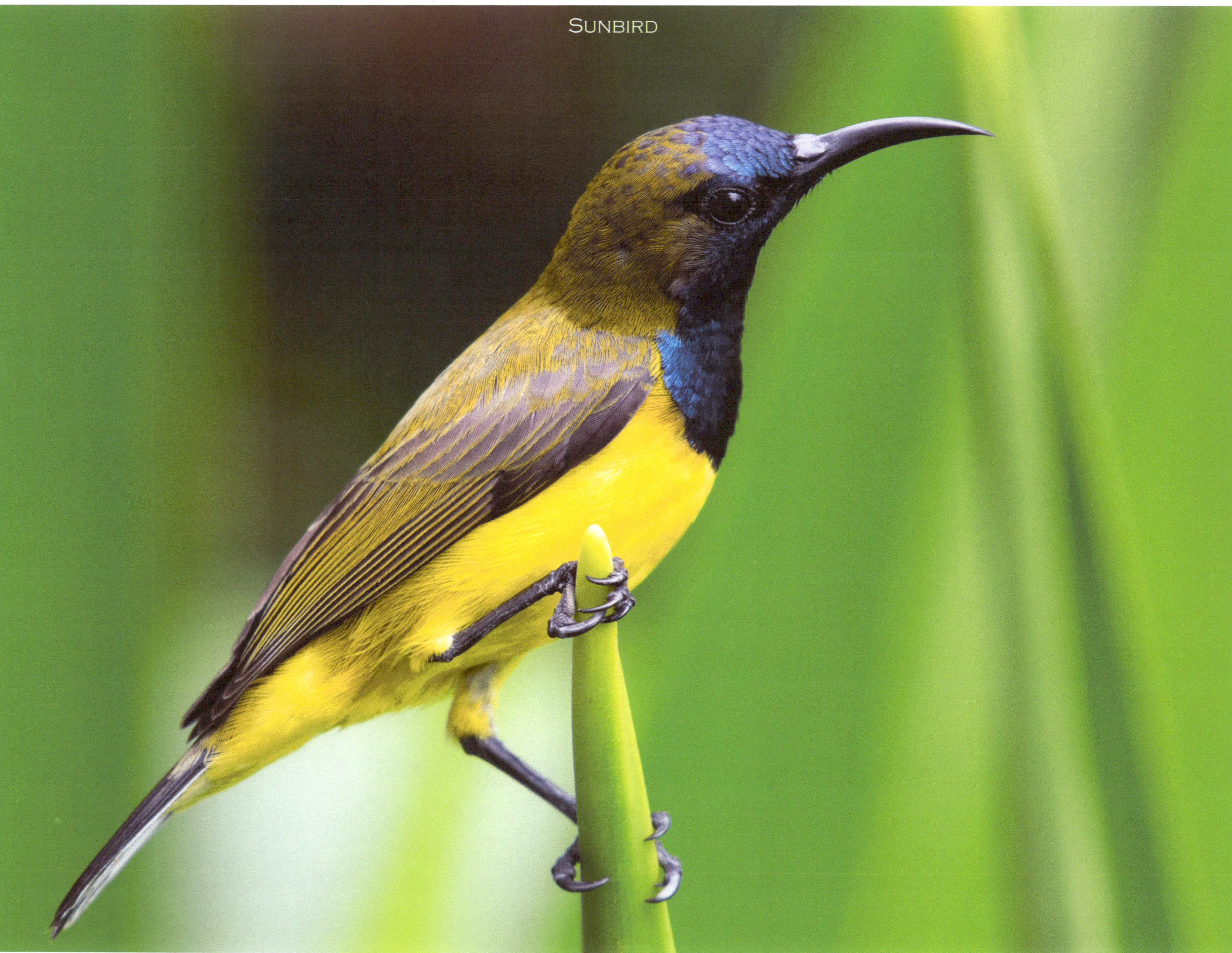

SUNBIRD

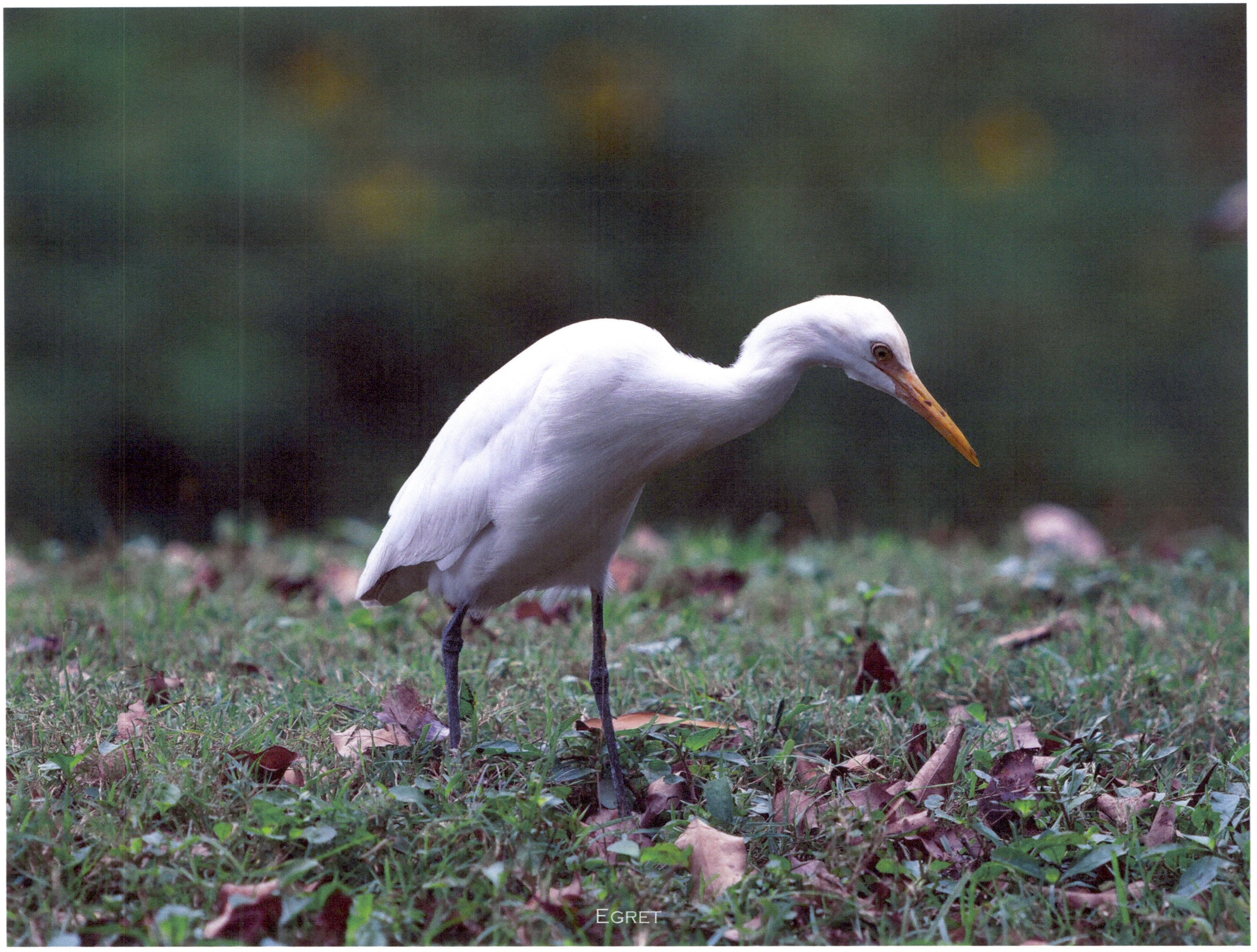

Egret

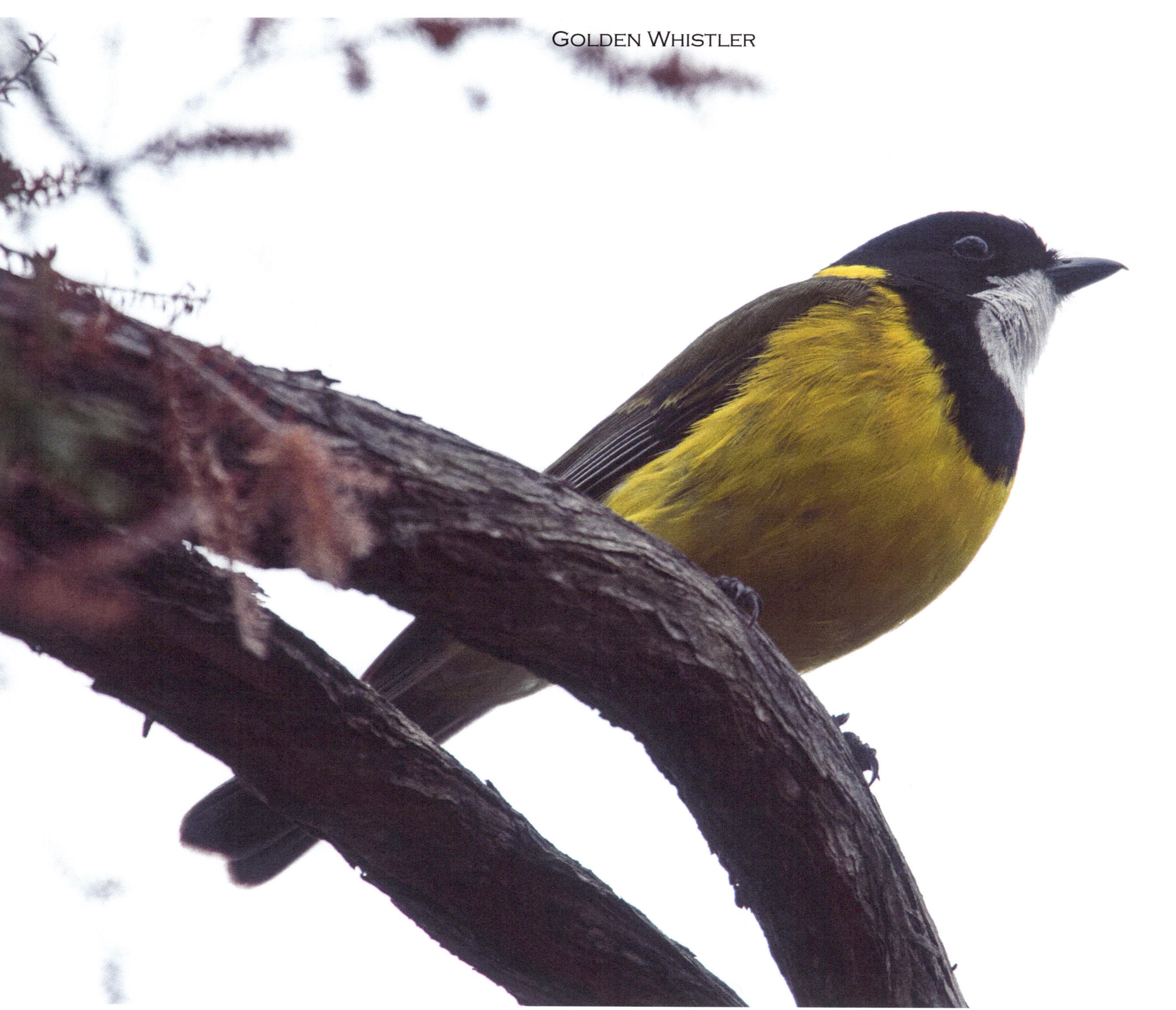

Golden Whistler

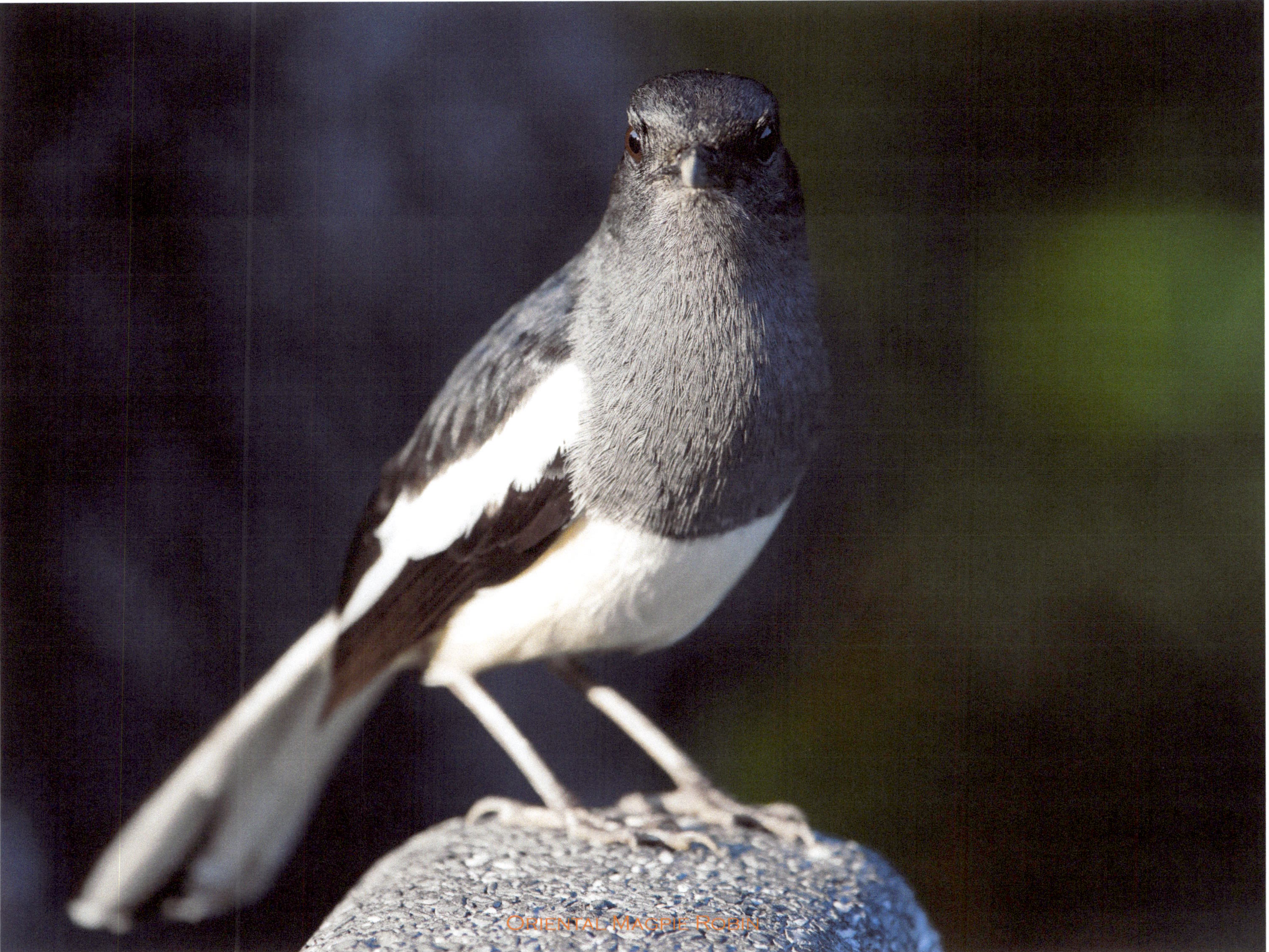
Oriental Magpie Robin

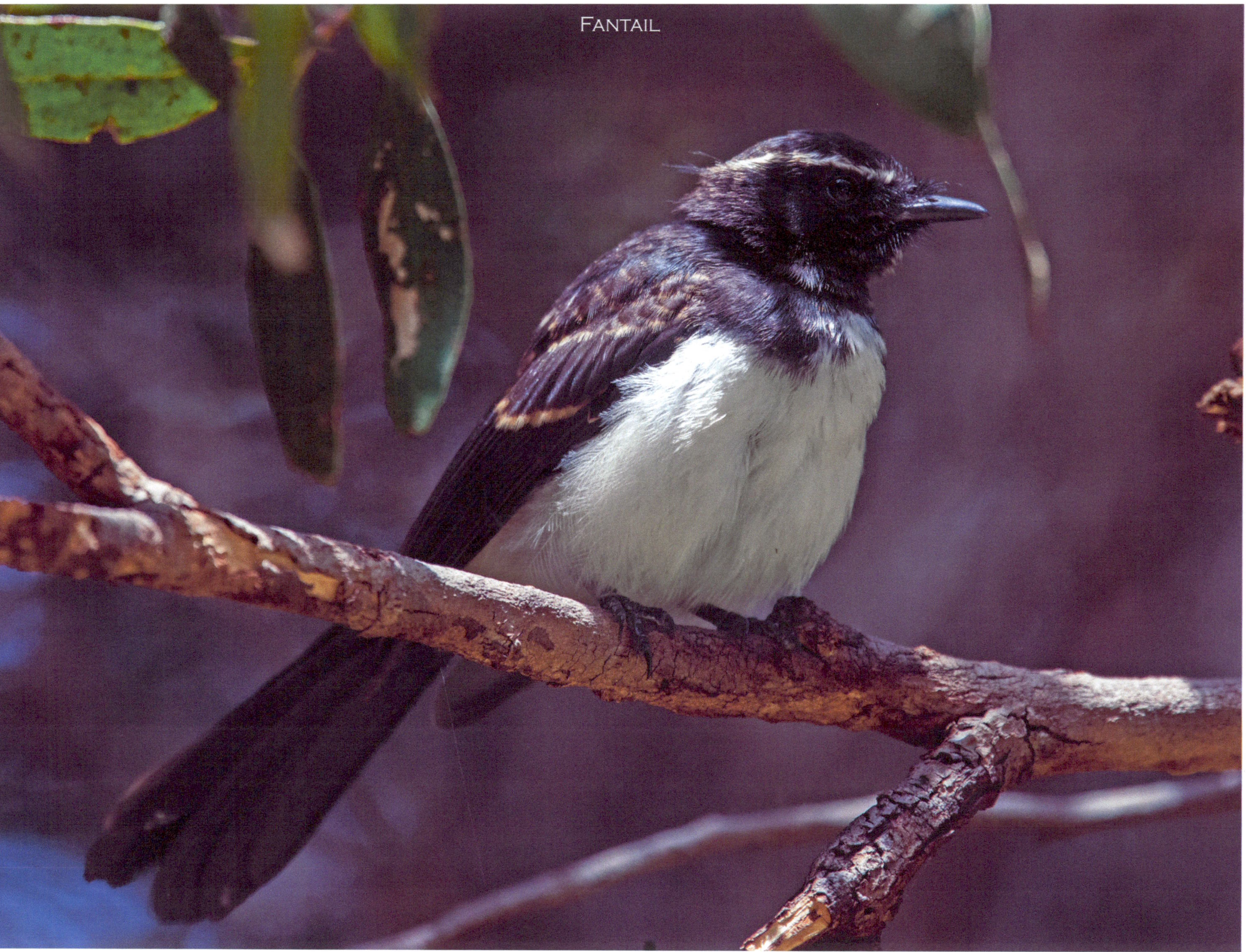

FANTAIL

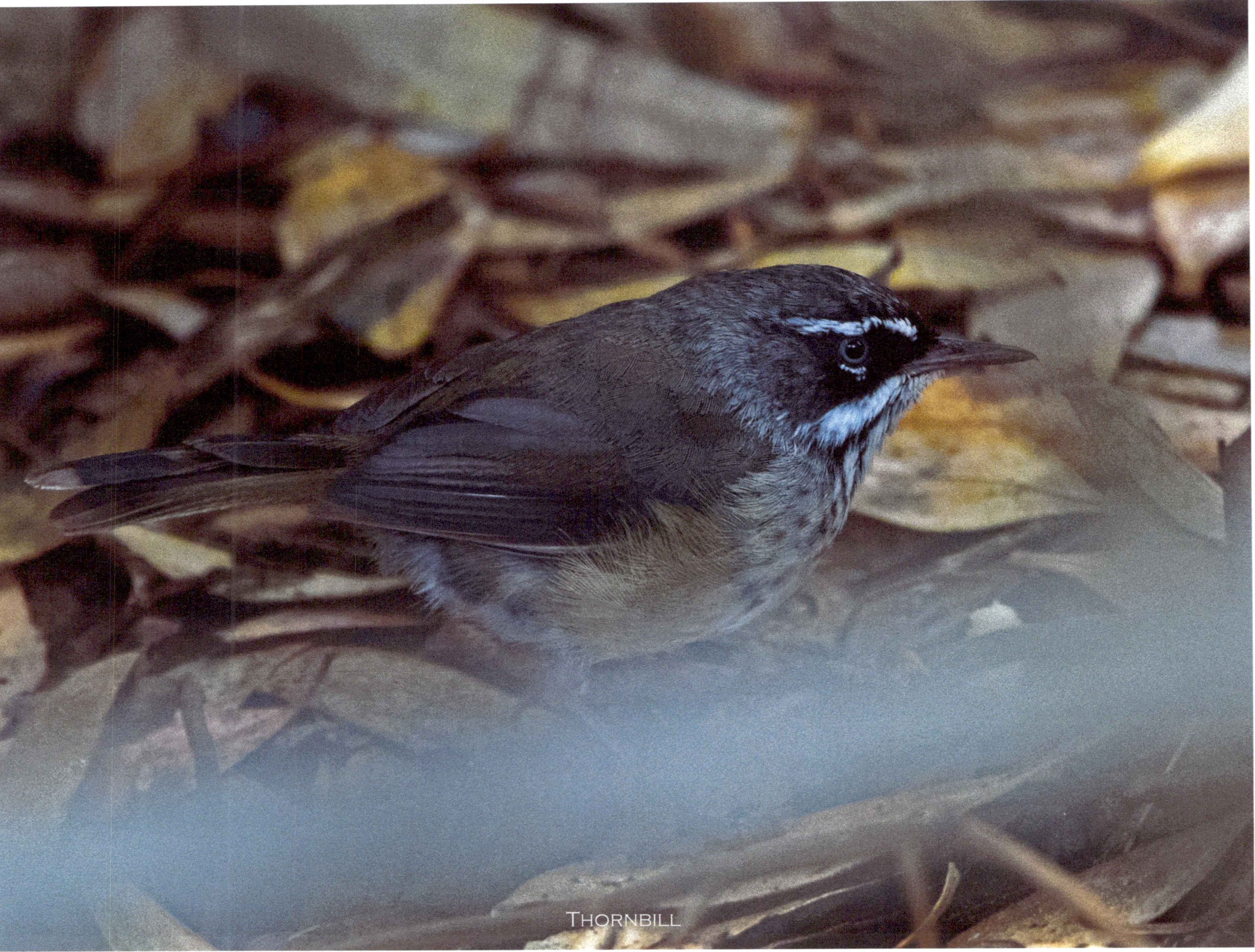

THORNBILL

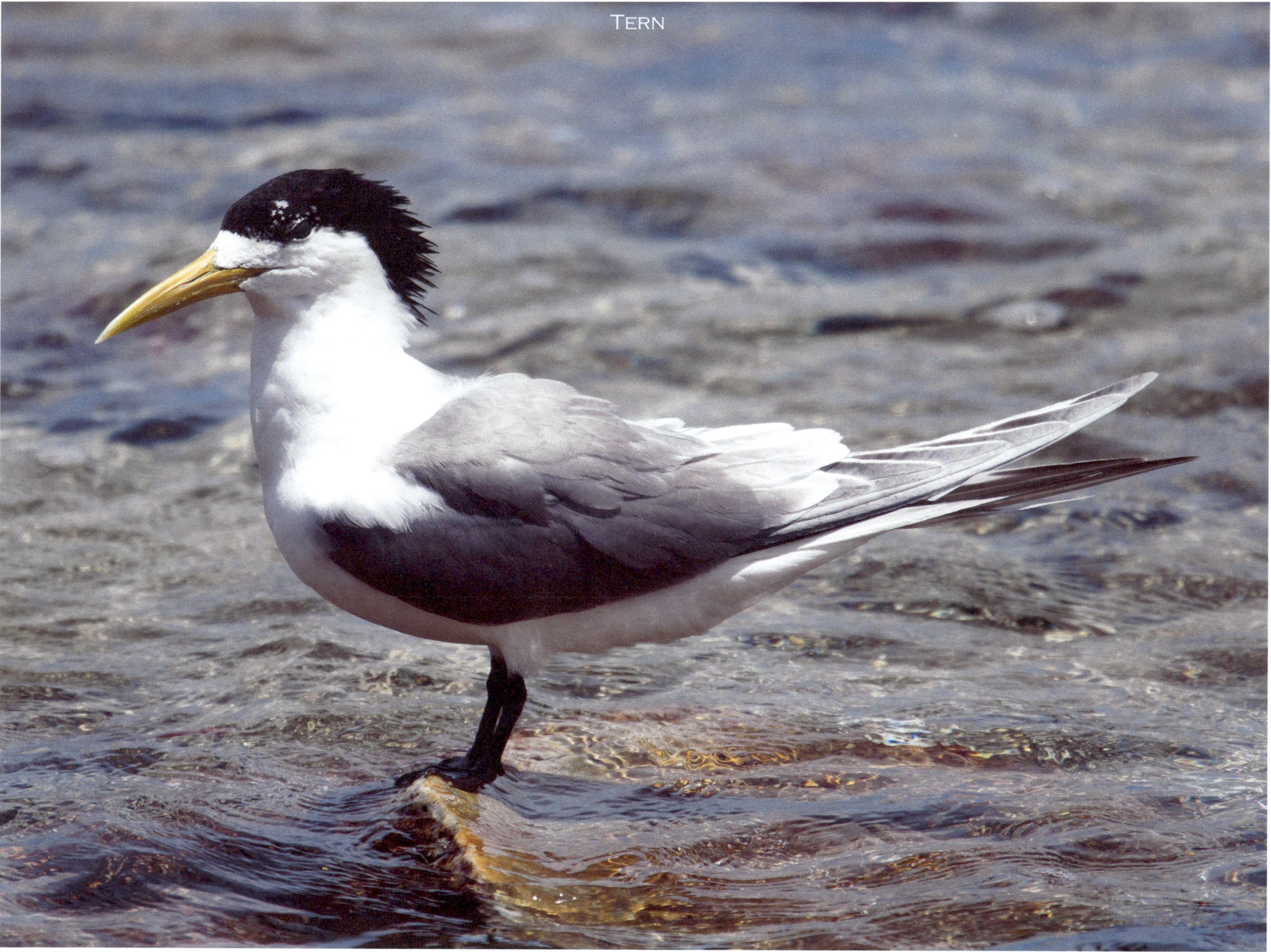
Tern

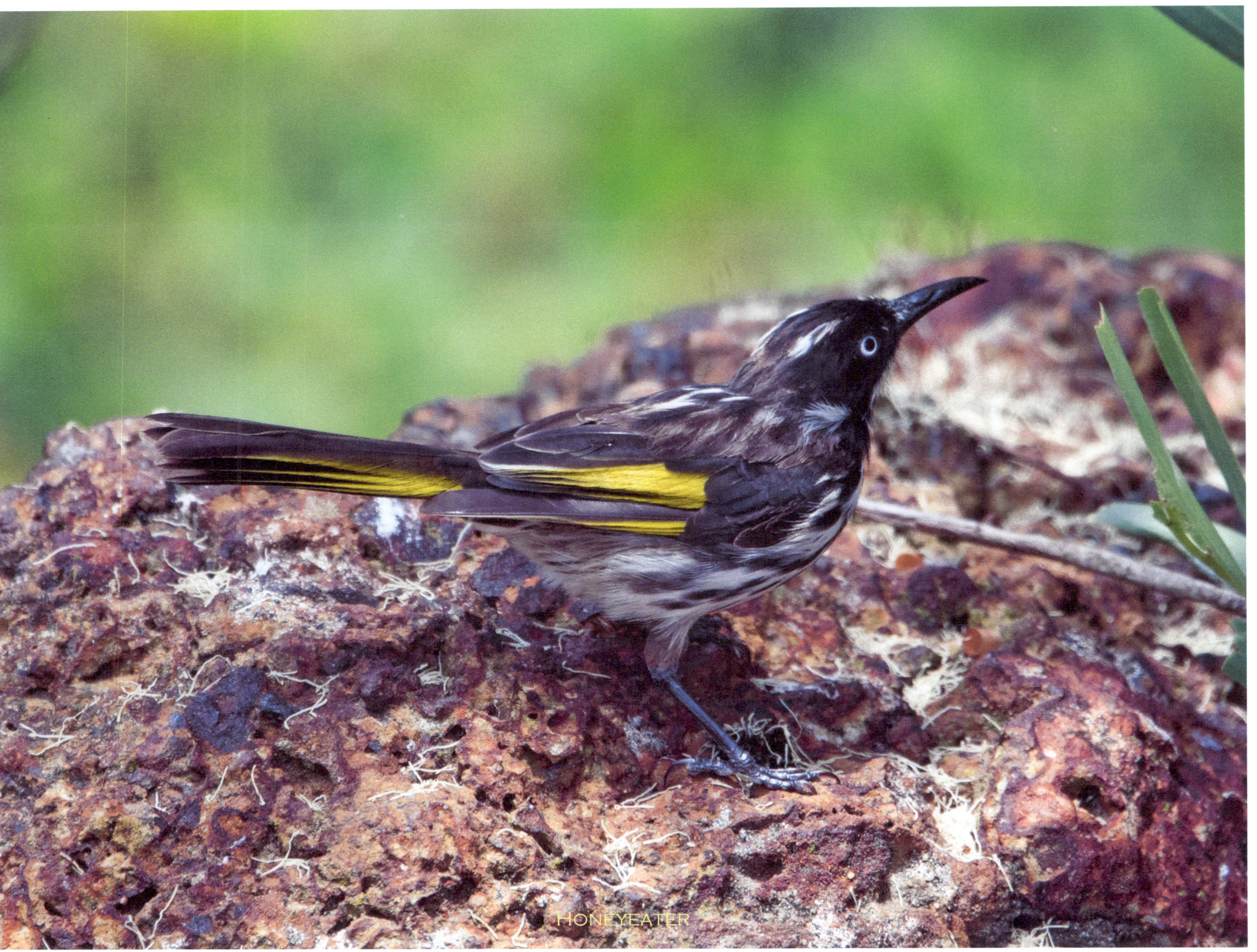
HONEYEATER

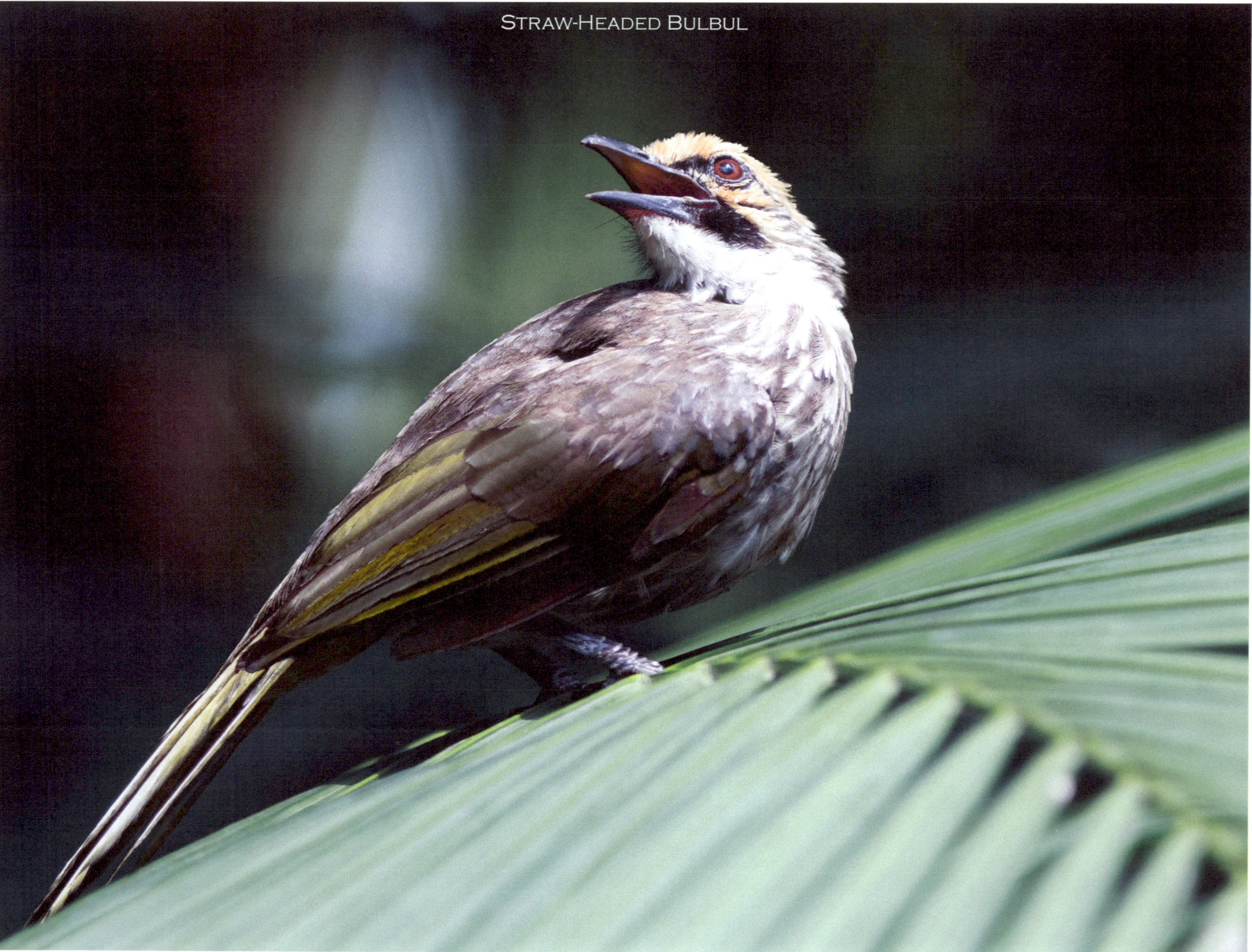

Straw-Headed Bulbul

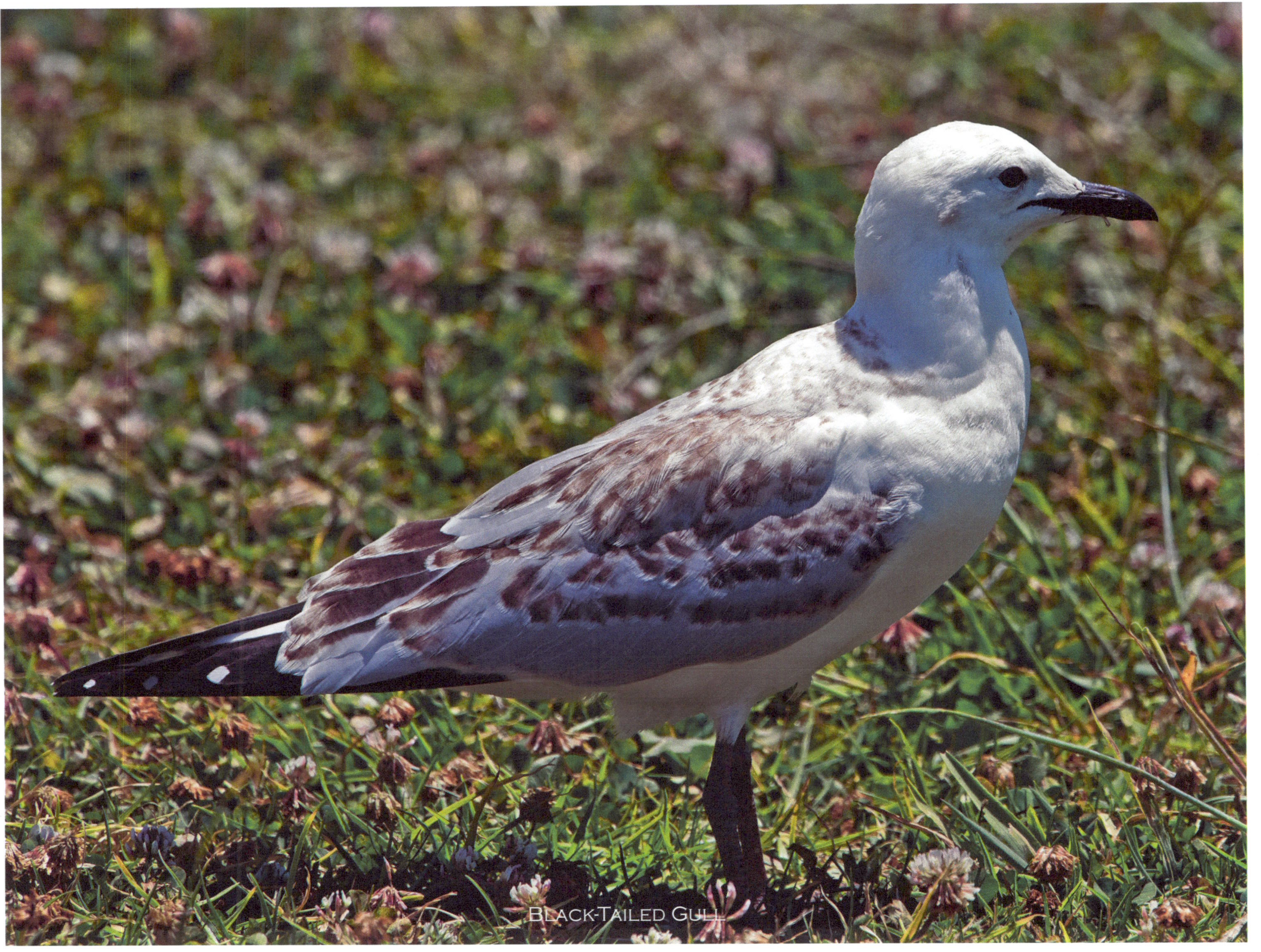

Black-Tailed Gull

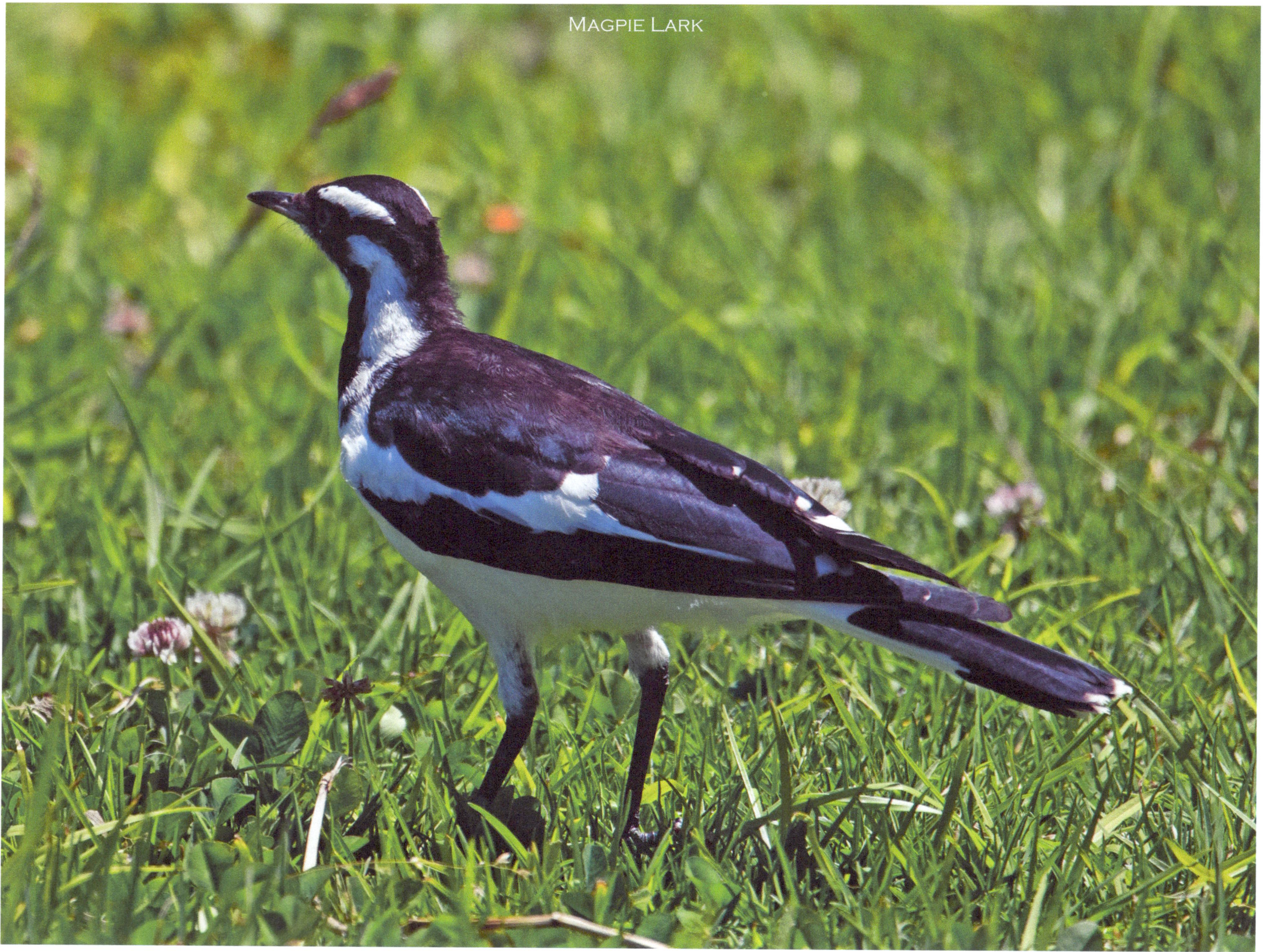

Magpie Lark

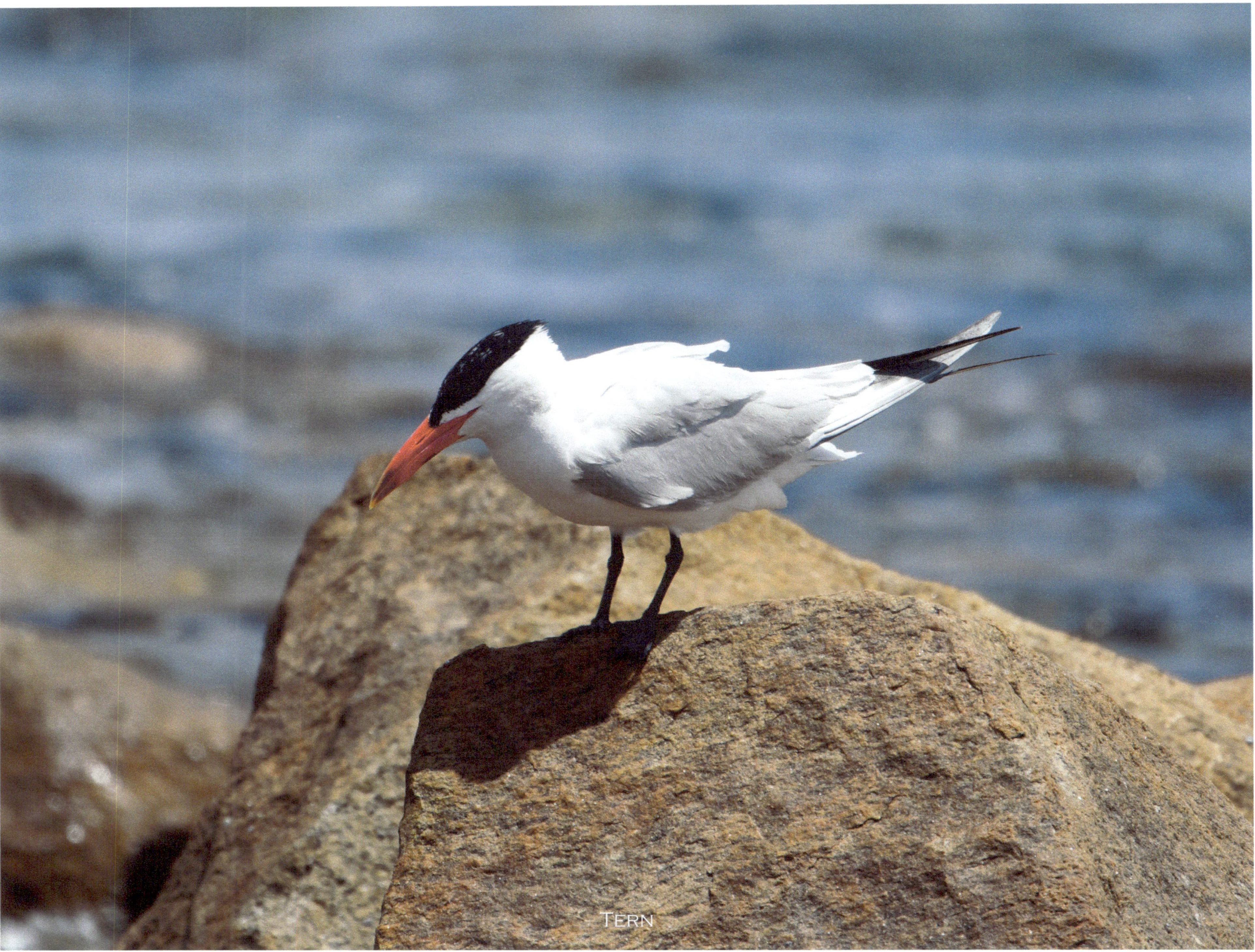

Tern

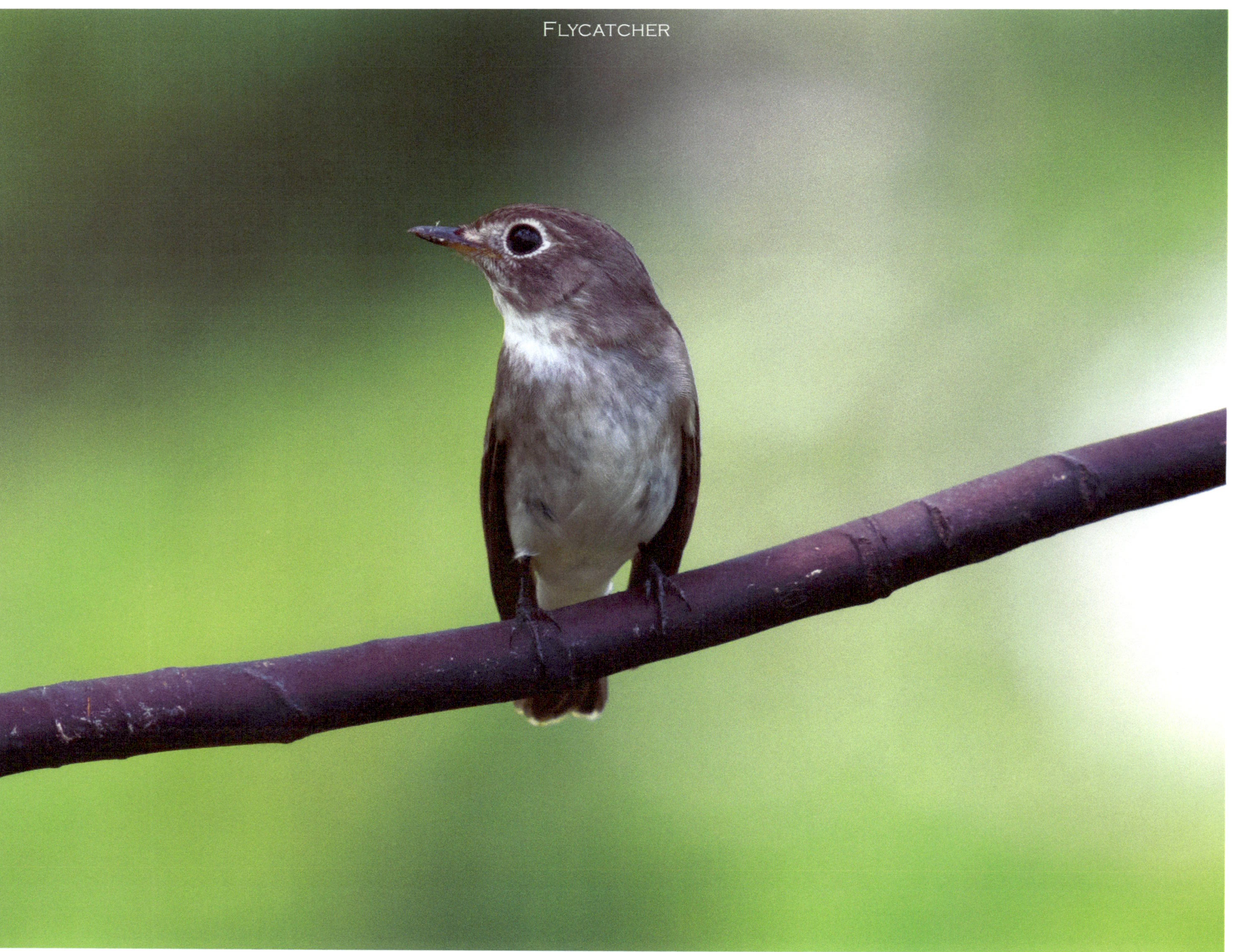

Flycatcher

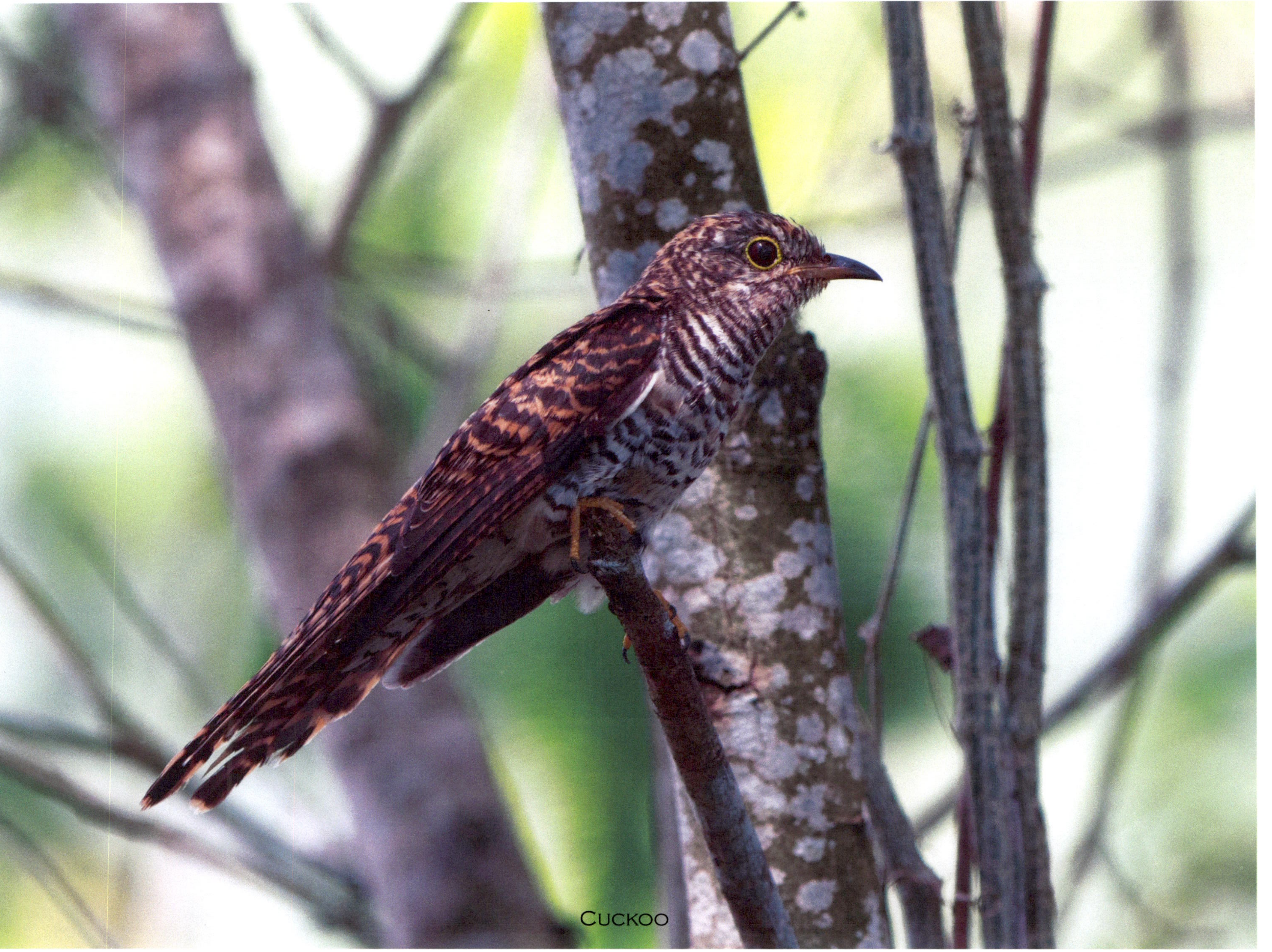

Cuckoo

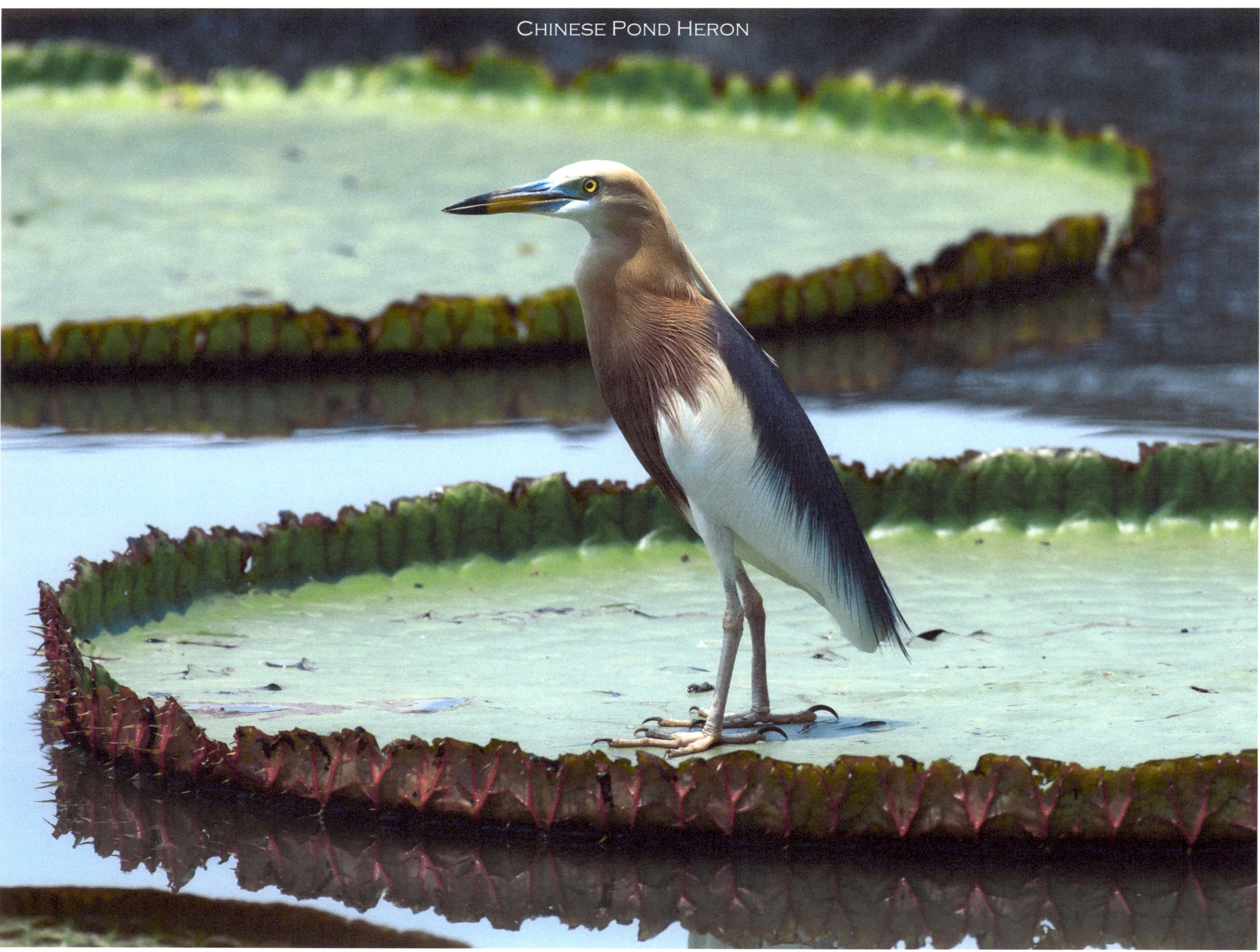
Chinese Pond Heron

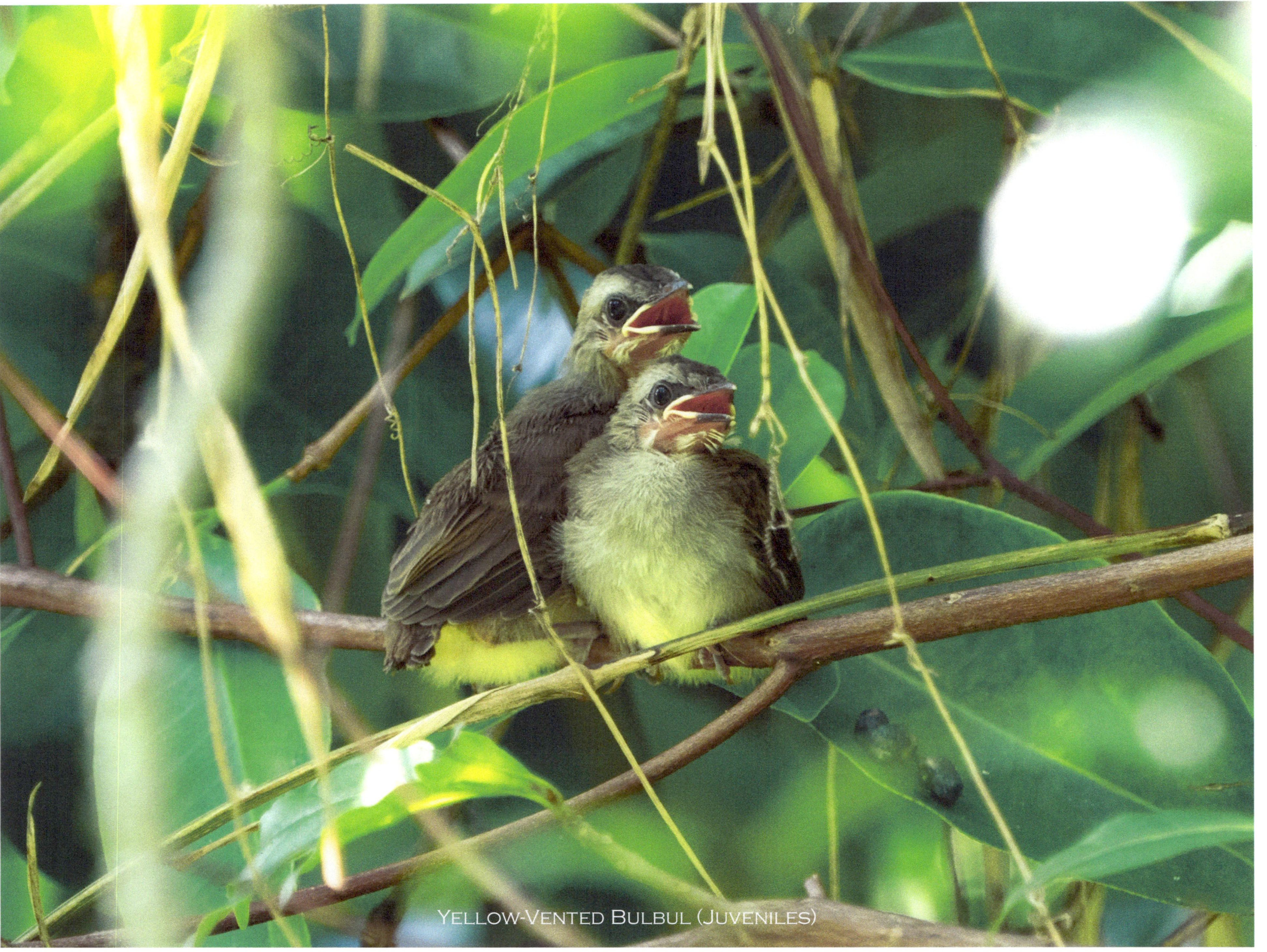

Yellow-Vented Bulbul (Juveniles)

Straw-Headed Bulbul

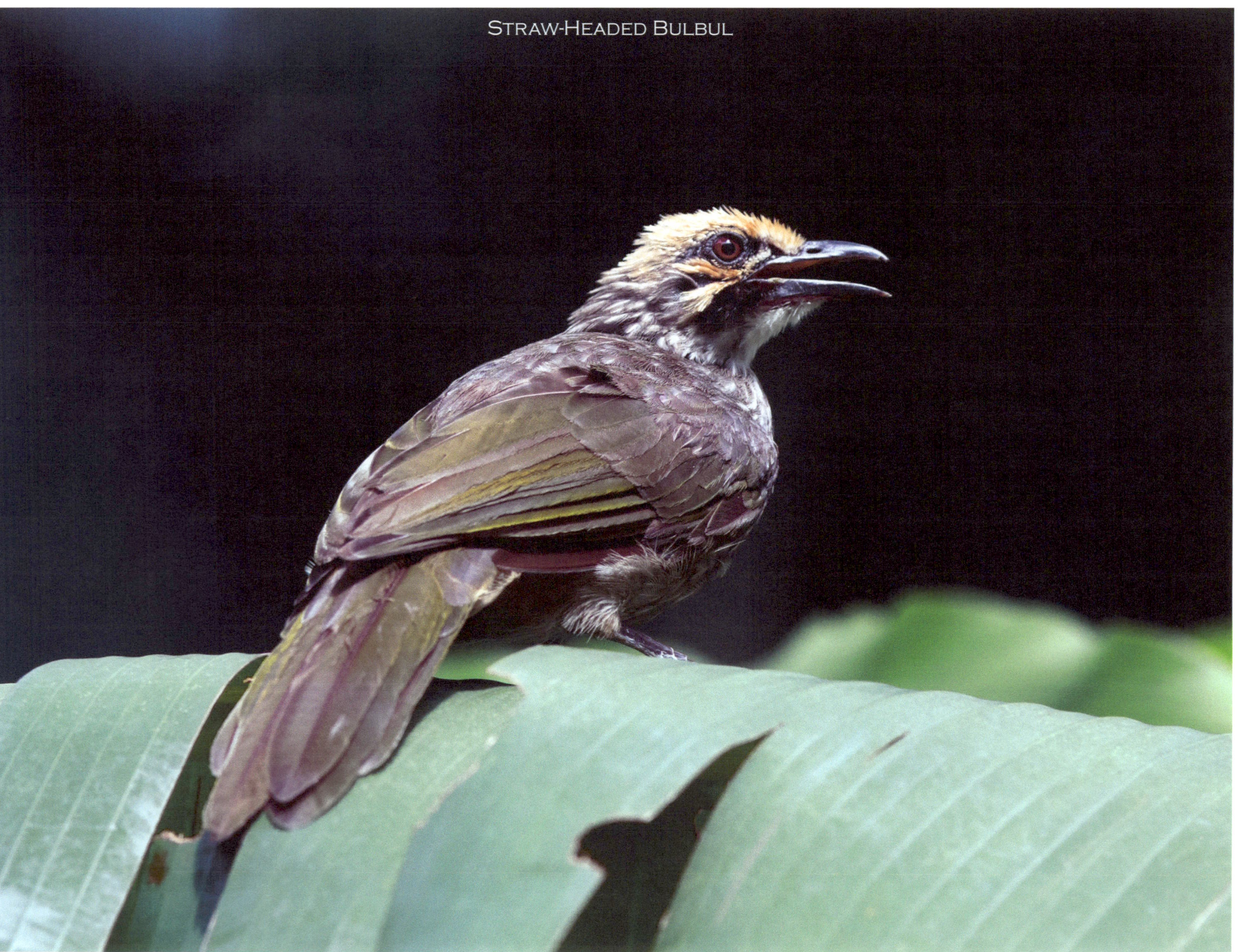

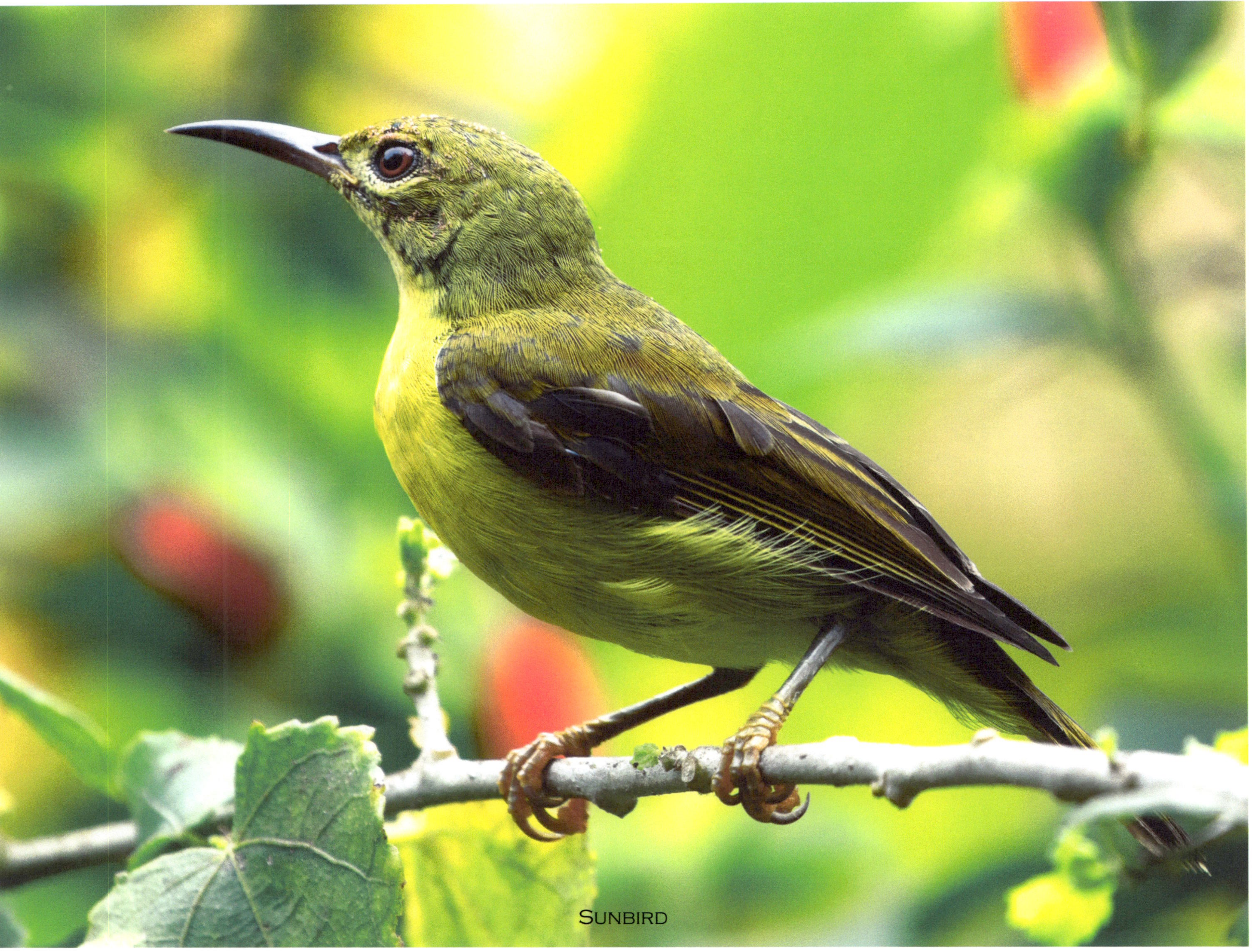

Sunbird

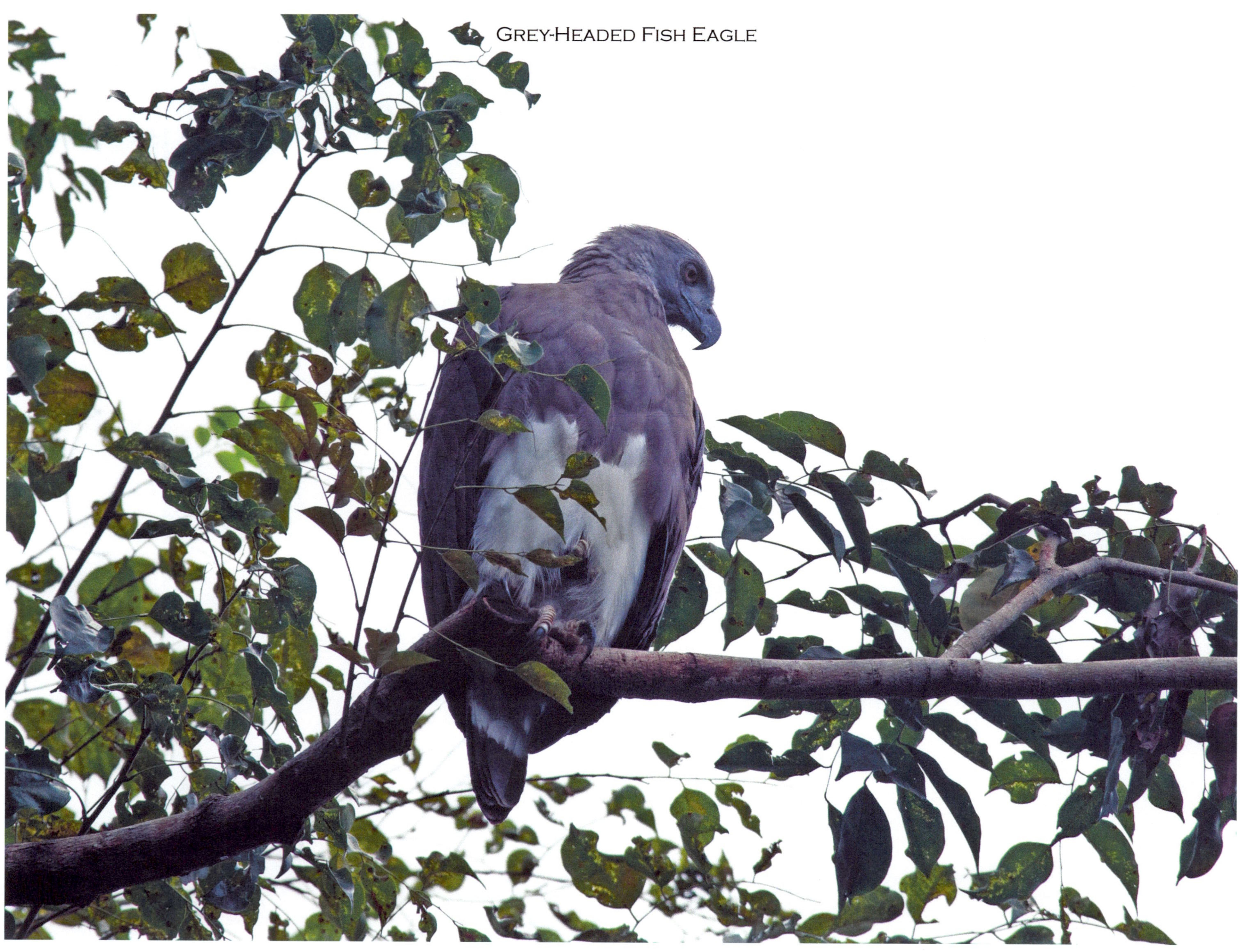

Grey-Headed Fish Eagle

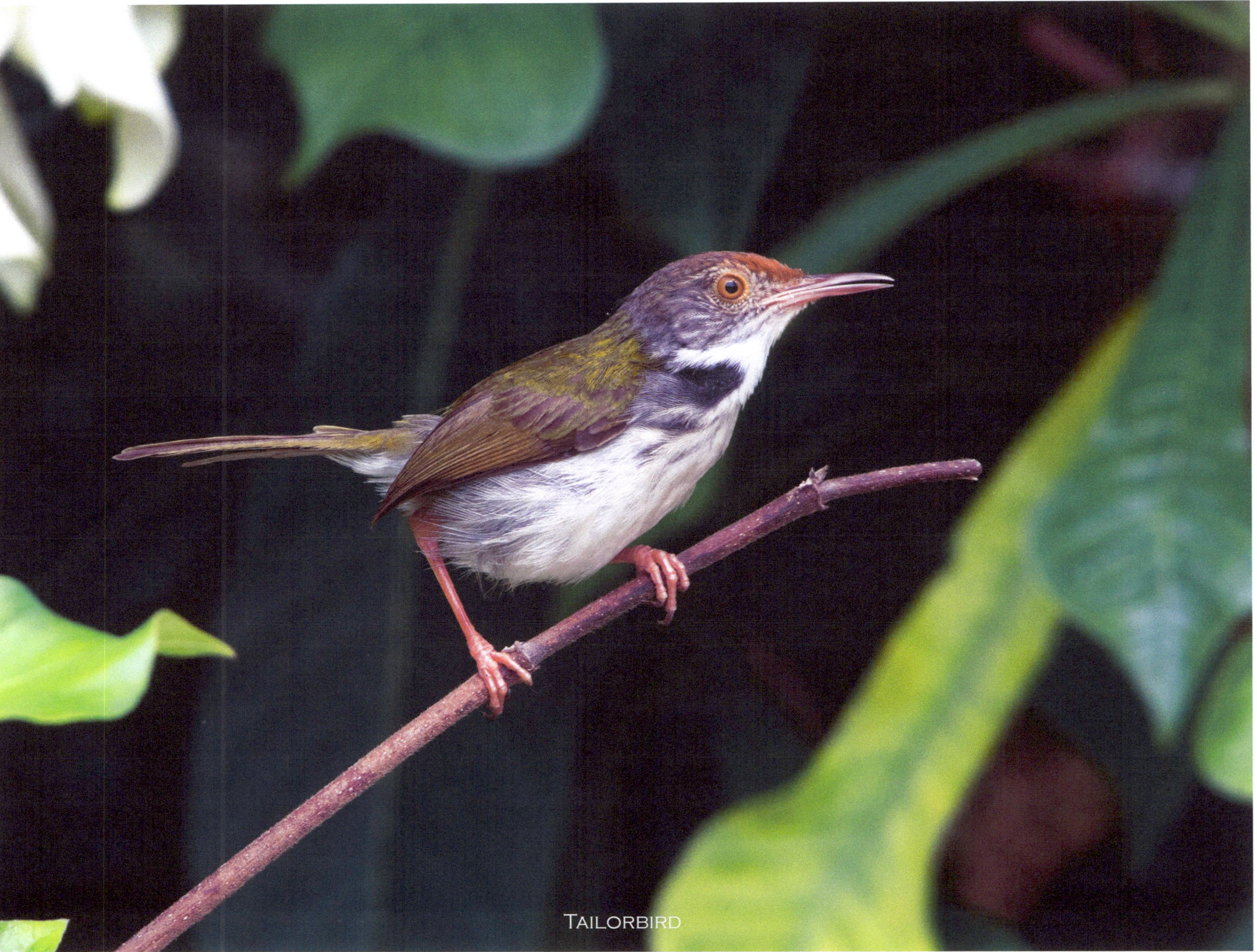

TAILORBIRD

www.ingramcontent.com/pod-product-compliance
Lightning Source LLC
LaVergne TN
LVHW071631100826
845154LV00007BA/129

9780998068213